# TEACHING FOLK DANCING

# TEACHING FOLK DANCING

*Audrey Bambra and Muriel Webster*

*Theatre Arts Books   New York*

Published by Theatre Arts Books
333 Sixth Avenue/New York 10014

Printed in Great Britain

*Publishers note*: Wherever the term 'modern dance' is used in this
book it refers to British modern educational dance, a style of
movement taught in Britain that generally stems from the
theories and instruction methods of the late Rudolf Laban. . . .
The notation of dances given in the book are referred to as
'kinetograms'; in the United States these would more likely be
called Labanotation kinetograms or simply Labanotation. They
follow the movement notation method invented by Rudolf
Laban and developed by his followers at the Dance Notation
Bureau in New York and elsewhere, and described in Ann
Hutchinson's *Labanotation* (Second Edition, 1970). More about
movement notation may be learned from the Dance Notation
Bureau, Inc., 8 East 12th Street, New York 10003. Information
about Folk Dancing in general may be obtained from the
Country Dance and Song Society, 55 Christopher Street,
New York 10014.

# CONTENTS

# ACKNOWLEDGMENT

The number of acknowledgments which appear in this book gives evidence that the contributions of a host of interested and interesting people and groups have been vital to the collecting of the dances and their supporting folklore. Throughout the period given to assembling the material, the generosity of all who have been approached for assistance has been outstanding. Busy people have arranged meetings, gathered together groups of young dancers after the working day, written long and helpful letters and been consistently encouraging. They have sent details of music, of costume, of the correct pronunciation of titles and of their meanings. They have prepared kinetograms. Above all they have been patiently ready to explain the pattern and proper execution of the dances and to struggle manfully with the authors' limited French and German. Their kindness has extended to much personal hospitality, offering an insight into home life in the countries.

Such generosity is born of their immense concern for the folk traditions of their own country and their enthusiasm for sharing the knowledge. It has made the task of writing the book an enlivening experience. It has brought increasing conviction that national dances provide an unusually good starting point for the growth of interest and understanding of people of other countries.

It is impossible here to write the individual notes of thanks which alone could adequately express full appreciation. It is certain that without such heart-warming co-operation the book would not have been possible. Names are recorded with gratitude in the relevant national section.

No less thanks are due to those whose help has been more general. The encouragement of Miss Ann Hutchinson and Mr Rickey Holden has led to the inclusion of kinetograms. These have been prepared through the generosity of Madame Jacqueline Challet-Haas and Miss Naomi Stamelman. Many technical problems could have been overcome only with the co-operation of colleagues, and thanks are gladly offered to Miss Margaret Smith, Miss Varina Verdin, Miss Olga Napper, Miss Rita Arkley and to Mr Oswald Sykes, Mr Colin Peters and Mr Bob Gleave. Without the unfailing support, encouragement and practical help of Miss Bede Barford, who assisted in checking the manuscript, the book would never have been finished.

Readers will see for themselves how greatly the book owes its vitality to Miss Lorna Wilson's delightful illustrations which enliven steps, holds and patterns in a way that words, however descriptive, cannot do.

The photograph on page 35 is reproduced by kind permission of *Foto Horst*, Klagenfurt. The photograph on page 83 is reproduced by kind permission of Dora Stratou from her book The Greek Dances, that on page 101 is by courtesy of the Israel Government Tourist Office, London, and the one on page 61 by courtesy of Presse Océan, Ancenis.

*Eastbourne and*
*Edinburgh 1972*
                                        AJB and CMW

# INTRODUCTION

Folk dance, which was once an important part of the programme in many schools, has in recent years been less frequently included in the curriculum. Now that educational dance is well established and more clearly formulated, it is likely that teachers will again find time to teach the older boys and girls some of the social dances of other countries.

The authors are not knowledgeable folklorists, but interested amateurs whose enthusiasm has grown from enjoyment in joining in the dances of many nations. They believe that, to have full meaning, the dances must be seen in the context of their nation's folk tradition. They are dull and meaningless if taught as mere patterns of movement but are increasingly absorbing as the dancers discover more about costume, music, language and tradition. Today both young and old travel widely. The folk dance makes a fascinating study which enables the traveller to share part of the life of a nation and so begin to see into rather than solely to look at the land and its people.

To many readers the information and advice given in this book will seem elementary and obvious. It is purposely simple as it is intended primarily for those who have not taught folk dance before. The book seeks to give clear and direct advice to help teachers present the dances with as great a retention as possible of the native style, and to awaken interest in the diversity of dances not only between nations, but also within each nation. Since it is possible here to indicate only some of the richness of folk dance the book will succeed if it inspires the reader to further research.

# PART ONE

## Folk or national dance—
## Its place in education

The word *national* is the term most often associated with the dances of European countries. However, the term might well be queried. In Great Britain it is in popular usage when describing dances other than its own, which are usually called folk or country dances. In the book itself the terms *folk* and *traditional* will be used, as folk dances transcend national boundaries and there are few dances which are characteristic of a whole nation. For instance, Yugoslavia is a relatively recent name used to embrace several smaller countries, each with its own individual culture and dance. The dances of Alsace, once a province of Germany, bear little relation to those of other French regions, each of which has its own distinctive folk dances. Another reason for not using the word national is that it is often confused with national character dances which are composed by a teacher or class, based on traditional steps. Passing reference is made to this type of dance which is still popular, but which is outside the aim of the authors of this book, who seek to preserve and spread knowledge of the traditional dances of many countries. The term *regional* would have seemed more correct until it was realised, at a festival in a small village in Portugal, that its meaning was too wide. On inquiry as to how large an area the dances covered, the indignant reply was that these dances belonged to that village and to that village alone, as did the lace patterns and ceramic designs. The neighbouring village had its own dances and designs and would never display those of another village at a local festival.

Some folklorists might query the inclusion of the dances of Israel, claiming that the dances are of recent and known origin. Yet they have a certain claim to both the terms *folk* and *national* in the sense that dances have been used as one of the means of teaching people, drawn from many countries, about their common heritage in the new nation.

Having decided to use the term *folk dance* it is important to see how some of the experts have defined it. Douglas Kennedy, the inspirer of the English Folk Dance and Song Society, writes 'No longer is the idea of "folk" restricted to country culture evolved by peasants in the practice of their husbandry. It has application to ourselves, to our habits, some acquired in infancy, others picked up casually and unwittingly as life goes on: these unself-conscious, personal traits link up with the inherited, collective, unconscious behaviour—a behaviour which we share with our stock at family, local, regional and even racial levels.'[1] Sentiments not dissimilar are expressed in *The Dance* by John Martin. He divides dance into three types: dance for the dancer, for the spectator, for communication. He ranks folk dance in the first category as recreational, saying 'It offers an underlying emotional oneness to all men and sends them home re-invigorated with this common heritage of their race.'[2]

For the majority of people who simply want to dance, folk dancing will continue to be a popular activity. However, in education the place of folk dance is often questioned for two reasons; firstly, because it is not creative as is modern educational dance which plays an important part in many schools and clubs; secondly, because folk dance, which is obviously meant to be danced by men and women or by boys and girls, is often taught only to girls. If it is to become valuable, then it must be practised by the young and old of both sexes and taught by both men and women.

What is the place of folk dance in education today? Ted Shawn in *Dance We Must* considers that all forms of dance help us to live more rhythmically. He says that 'through rhythm we are in the closest contact with the universe' and points out how all movements in sport which are rhythmical are more satisfying.[3] In folk dance there is the external rhythm of the music which helps with its pulsating beat as well as the stimulus of dancing in the group, sharing its rhythm through the touch of the hand, the sight, sound and feeling of the partner or group moving as one.

Many great educators would add another equally important reason for the place of the folk dance. They remind us that learning takes place through feeling as well as through thinking, although too few schools and universities have recognised this in practice. From experience in teaching children and adults it is interesting to note that often the more academic the school and the more intellectual the individual, the more difficult it is to introduce any form of dance, except through the faculty of thought. The students must know just which foot to use first and where to put it before taking any action. It is obvious that good though their education has been in one sense, something basic has been omitted, the joy of learning through doing and feeling.

Consider now the particular reasons for including folk dance in education. There are two questions to answer:

Is folk dance part of a culture that is worth preserving for its own sake?

What is the value of folk dance to the individual?

It is generally accepted that a study of past cultures is an essential part of education. Take two examples. Physical geography explains how the earth has evolved. The subject is a fascinating one in itself, while the knowledge is also necessary to understand the changes in the earth today and to predict future movement. A study of history records and explains past events, at the same time revealing how some of these events have led to our present situation. Both subjects are valuable as they describe the past and relate it to the present. In schools, a study of folk dancing is not considered important, except perhaps for its own sake. Few would claim that much could be learnt about modern countries through folk dancing, and it would certainly be difficult to prove this in factual terms. However, further thought will reveal how much it might teach about the past and present.

In many countries, particularly in some rural areas, folk dance has continued virtually unchanged for several centuries. It is probably danced only on high days and holidays but the dances themselves are little altered and there is no question of their being forgotten. In other countries folk dance is indeed a forgotten art, and the majority of people would be unable to demonstrate a single dance. In many areas the dances were lost and then revived and flourish today, either self-consciously or vigorously, often encouraged by the state for the purpose of tourism. In small pockets of Europe folk dance is carefully preserved and cherished in order to keep the unity of certain ethnic groups which are living in new political settings. Many of the dances which have been preserved are beautiful to watch and exciting to dance, but only recently have various groups realised how much their dances are appreciated when demonstrated to people of other nations. At this moment

there is a tremendous revival of folk dancing in Europe and it is relatively easy in some countries to learn the dances, although difficult to assess how much they have been embellished for purposes of demonstration. In much of Europe folk dance is definitely a vital part of the culture of a country, although its nature has to be appraised rather carefully.

In his studies on personality development, Daniel Prescott advocates 'the use of all the arts to bring children into the stream of our own culture, to aid them in appreciating how the present has grown out of the past', to help people 'in understanding and appreciating contemporary cultures'[4]. One cannot claim that by studying the dances of a country one therefore understands the country or the people. It would depend greatly on how deep and inclusive the study had been. If a class worked on a school project including the study of the history, geography, music, art and folk dance of one particular country, then this class might well have a better understanding of the culture of that country, of which folk dance is one aspect. Movement is an expressive art and the dances are derived from primitive and seasonal roots. It would therefore seem important for a country to preserve this rich aspect of its culture even if the dances are no longer the natural expression of young people. A study of historical dance could teach much about the various periods in history; a study of folk dance which has not changed, would give insight into the people and their origins.

The response to the first question leads to that of the second, the value of folk dance to the individual. If it is agreed that dance is part of a cultural heritage, then surely young people as individuals should learn some of the dances of their own country. It would be a great pity if the Highland and Morris and Sword dances with their local traditions were not handed down at least to the boys of the district. It would be equally sad if the English, Scottish and Irish country dances were lost to future generations. In a discussion group at a recent international conference, one of the subjects suggested for discussion was 'The Value of Folk Dance in Education'. As only the British thought the subject controversial it was not pursued. The other Europeans were so convinced of the value of teaching folk dances to their young people that they could see no possible debate.

As well as handing on one's own country's dances, it is important to learn the dances of other countries because of their particular interest and because they show one's own dances in perspective. Many Scottish and Irish dancers may be unaware that it is only their dances that are danced on the balls of the feet with toes extended as in ballet. A wide experience of the dances of other countries is exciting. An extra incentive is added as there are so many chances to study them at first hand, either at local festivals or on television.

An important part of the answer to those who question the value of folk dancing for the individual is that it is fun to do. One has only to watch some of the dances to appreciate the sense of national pride as well as the enjoyment of sheer physical skill that folk dancing gives to the experts. The pride and enjoyment are no less when one sees the ordinary people dance at a local festival or on the village green. It is obvious that there is a great exhilaration in dancing together and in sharing, even if unconsciously, the pride in a common past.

It is very usual nowadays for a school or a class to visit another country and much study goes into the preparation for such a visit. It would be good if a British group could not only show some of its own dances, but was also conversant with some of those of the host country. Links are then forged, as they would be if the two groups knew each others' songs, so that they can sing and dance together. The same applies to the individual who travels abroad. It was certainly true when we were able to join in the dancing of Kalamatianos, a Greek dance well-known in Cyprus. Afterwards some of the group insisted on speaking to us in Greek. They took it for granted that because we knew their dance language we must also know their verbal one. It was obvious, too, the pleasure that it gave to the dancers and watchers to realise that their dances were known abroad.

Having discussed the part that folk dance plays in the general and social education of the individual, consider now how it contributes to education in movement. All forms of dance affect the movement ability of the learner in varying ways and to different degrees (which is not the purpose of this book to appraise). Modern educational dance increases the awareness and understanding of movement to a high degree if it is well taught. Folk dance, especially if the dances of many countries are experienced, also contributes to sensitive bodily action and particularly to a sense of spatial awareness and to a certain type of rhythm and co-ordination. It has limitations as regards total body movement as, in the simpler dances, the amount of body movement is negligible. However, although there is little actual movement there is a

great deal of difference in the amount of body tension when performing a subtle Greek dance and a vigorous Austrian. In some of the more difficult types of folk dance such as Spanish, Hungarian, Russian and those of many eastern countries, a great deal of skill and subtle movement are demanded. The hand movements, the head and neck movements and sinuous hip action have to be studied for many years before the student can approach perfection. Some of the American modern dancers such as Ruth St Denis have made a particular study of oriental dance and this influence was apparent in subsequent productions. Certainly the modern and folk dance should complement one another. Just as the study of a second instrument contributes to the musicality of the musician, so should the study of two forms of dance help the dancer. Folk dance taught by a good teacher of modern dance or ballet who is also knowledgeable about folk dancing, should be able to offer a second approach to dance. This approach would be welcomed by the less creative or less skilled teenager whose confidence and enjoyment in movement might be increased.

Folk dance has, therefore, a positive contribution to offer in education and recreation. Because movement is an expressive art and the dances belong to an eternal past, the student of folk dance may gain insight into the temperament and *mores* of a group or nation. Folk dance has a part to play in movement education and, above all, it is an age old activity that most people of all ages still enjoy doing.

References
[1] Douglas Kennedy, *English Folk Dancing Today and Yesterday*, G Bell and Son Limited, London, 1967, page 38
[2] John Martin, *The Dance*, Tudor Publishing Co, New York, 1946, page 28
[3] Ted Shawn, *Dance We Must*, Dennis Dobson, London, 1946, page 10
[4] Daniel Prescott, *Emotions and the Educative Process*, American Council on Education: General Conclusions to the Study

# PART TWO

## General principles

Many people think that it is easy to teach folk dancing. They believe that since the steps and formations are laid down by tradition it is only a question of following certain directions. Yet verbal instructions are but the bare bones of dance and, even if these are carefully followed, do not ensure that the style and character have been interpreted intelligently. Only a teacher with some knowledge of folk dance in general and a deeper knowledge of the dances of some countries in particular will succeed. Experience both in dancing and teaching is essential, and a start must be made by learning from first-hand material as well as from books. The latter are specifically valuable in refreshing the memory and in giving extra material about countries of which the teacher already has some knowledge.

A good teacher will hope to teach the steps of a dance in the style of the country and in an atmosphere suited to folk dance. In setting out to do this, the following three issues must be considered.

In the first instance, the teacher needs to give a vivid impression of the particular style without imposing her own movement tendencies upon it. It is, for example, very difficult for a Scot not to show some of the characteristics of Scottish dance, the extended foot and outwardly rotated hip, both of which would be out of place in the dances of almost any other country. The best answer is for the teacher to have danced the dances, if possible, with the people of the country or with an expert in that particular style.

Secondly the teacher must develop in the class a good quality of movement and a high standard of dance without losing interest. This difficulty is not insuperable and the section entitled *The Teaching of Steps* should help the less experienced teacher or leader. It is very important that every practice should really be danced and enjoyed.

Thirdly, the teacher needs to consider how to create in a time-tabled period the social atmosphere which is the very essence of folk dance. This is a problem which cannot be entirely solved except in a recreational club. Folk dance should be picked up in a community, the young people watching the adults dance and joining in when ready. In an English village in which the traditional Morris or Sword dances are preserved, one novice, without verbal teaching, is usually carried through the intricacies of the dance by a team of experts. In a social club in Austria, newcomers and foreigners were taken through some of the simpler dances, partnered by the ablest dancers. This method is used to advantage in folk dance clubs or in recreational classes in which there is a mixture of able and inexperienced dancers. In a school, in which the teacher alone has knowledge, other ways must be found and suggestions are given in the section entitled *A Social Approach*.

An added difficulty in fostering the right classroom atmosphere is that most folk dances are intended for both men and women, and yet it is not customary to have mixed classes for dance in a secondary school. There are signs of change here, however, and it may soon be usual to have folk dance as an optional subject for both boys and girls. Mixed classes offer a natural social setting as well as allowing a greater range of dances to be taught. It is possible to teach couple dances to girls only. However, the fact that in recent years chain dances seem to be more popular seems to suggest that many girls do not enjoy having to dance as boys. Now that folk music has become very popular the time seems ripe to introduce dances to the folk club evenings. The first approach may be a request to the folk dance band to accompany some folk dance on a particular occasion; from then on a few dances might be introduced to the weekly meetings until they become an accepted part of the programme. In women's recreational classes where folk or national dance is popular it is hoped that men may be invited occasionally so that folk dance ceases to be merely a part of Keep-Fit.

## Selection and use of material

### PLAN FOR THE TERM
Before preparing a single dance lesson it is necessary to think ahead so that a course of lessons, perhaps lasting for one term, may be planned. There is no one right way of doing this as the dances selected will be based on the teacher's particular knowledge as well as

on the needs of the class. The following methods used both by teachers in schools and by leaders of recreational classes offer scope for discussion.

## 1 Unplanned lesson

The dances are selected lesson by lesson without any overall plan in mind beyond the knowledge that a certain record is available or that the dances can be taught without much preparation. Every teacher uses this method in a crisis, but if resorted to too often, then neither teacher nor class have the satisfaction of having accomplished anything. Dances so taught tend to have a certain sameness in style so that an observer would have no idea whether the dances were all from one country or from very different parts of the world. More important still, the dancers themselves may be equally ignorant. The music might give an indication but on the whole such lessons consist of a series of activities in which steps and formations are learnt without any background. This is neither dance nor education.

## 2 Improvisation on basic steps

With this approach the teacher selects a country and gives the class a vocabulary of steps taken from several dances of that country, possibly stipulating that all the dances shall be based on one formation such as a couple or a chain dance. She then gives the class the opportunity to make up its own dances based on the steps taught.

Such a lesson is often enjoyed, especially if, because of the teacher's real interest in movement, the steps have been well taught. However, there are drawbacks. Sometimes the movement is too abandoned for women's folk dances which tend to be fairly restrained. The steps may not all be from the same region and so there may be a lack of integrity in what is taught as folk dance. Some years ago this type of dancing, referred to as national character dancing, was universally taught and was very popular. If, however, folk dance is worth teaching there is surely a moral obligation to teach as truthfully as possible. The teacher would probably never consider using this method when teaching the dances of her own country. Folk dance is not a good medium for creative expression, whereas modern dance surely is. Certain countries do make a feature of improvisation of steps led by the leader of the group, but he is usually so steeped in the knowledge of his regional dance that he can embroider steps and still retain their character. It is very difficult for a foreigner to do this.

This method, however, still has its occasional uses, especially if the dance is a gypsy dance from Italy or Spain. The gypsies pick up a great variety of steps as they wander from country to country and they devise some exciting dances.

## 3 Teaching by contrast

There are many ways of using contrast to heighten observation and understanding, and the following are but a sample.

*a* The teacher selects two or three countries which offer strongly contrasting dance styles, eg Austria, Greece and Rumania. She chooses perhaps three dances from each country or region, stressing the differences in movement styles, thus interesting the dancers in trying to show and feel the contrasts. Discussions about the reasons for the differences are valuable as long as sweeping statements are not accepted. Such truisms as 'all mountainous people dance high on their toes and use leaps in their dances, while people from flat countries use long travelling steps' are unacceptable. There is perhaps some truth in these statements but they need qualifying.

*b* The teacher decides on one formation, a chain, a trio or a longways dance and again selects from countries offering a good contrast in style within the same formations, perhaps the French *farandole*, a Serbian *kolo* or a Portuguese chain dance. It helps to show that it is the movement, not the formation that really indicates the character of a dance.

*c* The teacher uses a book or record to select dances as different as possible in style, step and formation. This is a very practical method in that the teacher, leader and students have all the material in a compact form. It requires good teaching if it is not to degenerate into a repetition of the weaknesses of the first method. In the future, the availability of film loops of the dances in question would be a tremendous asset to the teacher and sometimes also to the learner.

## 4 The study of one country

The teacher or leader decides that the class should be absorbed in the dances of one country for a course of lessons. Sometimes the choice is made because of her particular knowledge of a country where she learnt the dances at first-hand. It may be that the school visit has been arranged to Brittany and that she seizes the opportunity to teach the class about that region through its dances. There may be living in the area a group of Polish immigrants, knowledgeable about their own country's dances, who would invite her to their dance meetings or visit the class to give a demonstration of the real dance style. There is no doubt that by working over a period of time on one style dancers come closer to the real thing, especially if good use of first hand contacts have been made.

The school itself will be able to add to the knowledge of certain allied aspects of folk dance. This particular approach lends itself well to the setting up of a project in collaboration with other members of staff. They may be invited to come and see the dances, join in the discussion, contributing their specialist knowledge. If the project is a joint one then all would work on their particular aspects of the country in English, geography, history, art, music and dance. At the end of the study the class might arrange the hall with books and maps of the country or region, posters of the area, pictures of costume or dolls in authentic costume, musical instruments and records of typical dance music of the region. Members of the class would explain to an invited audience what they had been studying, show the dances and sing some folk songs. They might invite the members of the audience to join in some of the easier dances and songs so that they could share in the atmosphere as well as gain knowledge of the country.

5   *The study of a group of neighbouring countries*
This is a course particularly suited to recreational leaders, students, senior classes or clubs. It is much more difficult to express the subtle differences between the dances of the Scandinavian countries which may seem very similar than to work on obviously contrasting countries. The dances of the Balkans may seem to an outsider to have more similarities than differences but on closer study this is not so. Such studies need not only a very knowledgeable teacher, but also a class interested in the subtle differences in movement. Whatever groups are chosen the same methods may be used, but it is easiest to take as an example the study of the dances of England, Ireland, Scotland and Wales.

It allows clubs steeped in the dances of their own country to discover how differently their near neighbours dance. The knowledge of their own particular style can serve as a starting point to emphasize the contrasts. The course caters too for groups which are more knowledgeable about the dances of countries other than their own; it is quite usual to find groups of 'national' dancers very ignorant of the dances of their own country.

For groups only beginning folk dancing, it at least provides insight into the differing styles of dance in the British Isles. The teacher should see that a dance from the north of England such as the Morpeth Rant is included in order to show the slight similarity between the rant step and the Irish and Scottish jigs and reels. In a school or college this course may be planned in the form of a project or voyage of discovery in which individuals or groups try to discover some of the historical and cultural reasons for the differences.

The aim of the study would be the same, whether the dances were from Britain, the Mediterranean countries or from Alpine areas. The last group makes interesting study as more similarities are found in dances from the parts of Italy, Switzerland and Austria which border on the mountains than there are in other dances of the parts of the same countries far from the Alps. One aim of working in this particular region would be to find the similarities rather than differences, making a slightly different emphasis.

Whatever approach is chosen, two things are important. The first is that folk dance should not be studied in isolation. In a school this may be avoided by carefully setting up a project as described in *The study of one country*, also applicable when using other methods of approach. The dance teacher may merely be asked to produce some dances for a large school project or play and may have to alter her own work accordingly or the project may be planned as suggested. In recreational classes it may be helpful to bring in some experts from outside who have particular knowledge of certain aspects of the country. They might show films of the area and tell of their experiences in the country so that the dances are seen as part of a whole. Some members of the group might even decide to visit the country and study the dances at first hand.

The second matter of importance is to build up a repertoire of dances that the dancers know well and enjoy dancing. To qualify as well-known, the dancers should be able to recognise the music and immediately associate it with a dance that they are able to dance with the minimum of help from the leader. Too often dances are never brought to life again so that the class is not aware of the rich vocabulary of dances it has acquired and misses the fun of doing social dances which everyone knows. It may be very valuable for classes not academically gifted to perform to their other teachers something that they can do well. This helps to give them the confidence that they often need. There are various occasions that suggest themselves for revision of a known dance: sometimes to give zest or relief to a lesson in which a lot of new work has been taught; or to provide the ideal contrast to a newly taught dance. Occasionally the class may be invited to show selections from their repertoire to an audience.

This leads to the question of demonstrations which have great values and certain dangers. Folk dancing is meant to be danced and not watched, but there are certain times when it helps a class to bring its work to a climax and to realise that it is appreciated by an audience. There are occasions too when, in school and post-school work a demonstration is demanded for a particular purpose and the needs of an audience have to be considered. When preparing a programme it is important to provide contrasts in music, in formations and steps as well as in atmosphere. This is usually easy if many classes are taking part, but demands careful thinking ahead for a single recreation dancing group. The focus must be kept on the dancing itself, so that the audience is interested, but the sense of group feeling is not lost. Too often a demonstration produces dances so obviously prepared for an audience that it becomes a spectacular show rather than an honest folk dance festival in which the dancers are showing each other and the audience their carefully prepared dances. This sense of festival, illustrated well by both the English Folk Dance and Song and the International Folk Dance Society, helps to keep the real feeling of the dancers meeting together to dance.

The formal demonstration, with its carefully prepared entrances and exits and some solo work, is better suited to dance in its art form although there are occasions when the formal folk-dance festival has a place. It is quite usual to include some folk dances in a formal demonstration of modern dance or ballet. Here it is most important that the folk dances should retain their own character. When an Austrian dance is being shown, a group of German and Dutch dancers could be grouped around as if they were the audience. They would applaud and congratulate the Austrians and walk off with them, returning when it was their turn to perform. In effect the folk dance should be shown as part of a festival of dancers showing their dances to each other as well as to the audience.

Today, with the great interest in folk music shown by the young, it seems right to think more often in terms of folk evenings in which songs, music and dance are interwoven. Here the spectators may well join in some of the singing and dancing. Such occasions would help to link the folk song with the folk dance, would make a natural setting for both sexes to dance together, show other people what the folk group is doing and might increase membership.

THE PLAN OF A LESSON

While it is true that different age groups, different types of classes and different types of dances may demand varying lesson plans, it is also true that there are certain component parts of a lesson and certain principles which serve as a guide line for most situations. A lesson seems to divide itself naturally into three parts. For simplicity, these shall be referred to as introduction, practice, dance.

*Introduction*

A lesson should start the moment the first member of the class enters the room. While the others are still changing an atmosphere can be set, perhaps by the playing of the music of last week's dance which some will remember and show the others. Or, music for the new dance may be played and members of the class encouraged, as they come in, to move to it with any simple steps that the music may suggest. Once the dancers have used the space in the room and have warmed up to a feeling of dance, the first part of the lesson develops naturally with the introduction of simple new steps or the revision of steps already taught.

A great deal is learnt from a good demonstration. The teacher may either show the same steps several times, emphasising a new point when she sees that it is needed. Alternatively, she may show several simple steps, moving on to the next when the dancers have felt the rhythm of the step through repetition. Rhythm and repetition are the keynotes of this part of the lesson. At this moment the finer points are not being stressed except through demonstration. This is the time for doing and dancing with the minimum of standing still and talking. The teacher will use her voice as the class is dancing. The music, the sight of the whole step well danced, the opportunity to dance with the teacher and to repeat a step until it becomes part of the dancer, are the ways of learning that give satisfaction at the beginning of a lesson. Difficult steps, which require analysis, should be reserved for the middle part of the lesson.

Before moving to the next part of the lesson it is sometimes a good idea to bring the dancers together to tell them about the dance, the music, the costume and to show a map of the country; anything, in fact, that would help to place the dance in its context. A discussion is more acceptable after there has been a chance to move freely to the music. There can be no fixed rule about this, and many teachers like to describe the country before the teaching starts. It is also important that the dancers should learn how the future lessons are to be planned.

*Practice*
Details of this section are given under *The Teaching of Steps*. The dancers know the plan of the lesson and something about the dance and should therefore be prepared to work knowledgeably at the difficulties. The teacher sets to work to improve the steps danced earlier and to teach the difficult steps that are required in the dance. Now is the time for analysis of steps, especially for those who learn best by this method. The rhythm of the step should be kept in mind, even during analysis, and the voice used in a slower rhythm until gradually the step is mastered and the music brought in to help. It may be necessary to practise the step turning alone or with a partner so that everyone is conversant with each step in all the forms that the dance demands. The practices should be presented in as interesting a way as possible so that they are enjoyed for their own sake. The steps must be learnt from the start in the style and character required. Too often it is thought that the step pattern can be taught first and the style added later, but the two cannot really be separated.

*Dance*
The dance should be developed gradually, each figure being repeated and improved before the next is added. After two figures have been learnt, they should be joined and repeated until the two figures flow naturally into one another. Only then should the third figure be introduced. One of the most common mistakes of an inexperienced teacher is to rush through a dance too quickly with the good intention of polishing it later. This the class is often unwilling to do as, by its standards, the dance is now learnt. The dancers are willing to dance it for fun but are not interested in improving it. On the other hand, too slow progress is also disastrous to enjoyment which should always be the climax of a dance lesson. During the performance of the actual dance, the teacher should be prepared to lose some of the finer skill acquired during practice.

The character may be improved by reference to the people whose dance is being learnt; their sense of pride and posture, the warm climate which tends sometimes to produce a less energetic style, a more relaxed movement or a slower rhythm. All these points help to improve the style in a way that is not considered to be a reversion to step practice.

To sum up, in every section of the lesson there should be a feeling of dancing. During step analysis this will be momentarily lost but it must be recaptured immediately the step is learnt so that all practices are danced. It is more important to capture this sense of dance than it is to achieve precise steps and figures. A teacher must not expect the sense of dance to appear with the final dance unless she has fostered it earlier.

The following situations: the teaching of beginners, the social approach and the teaching of chain dances, will demand some variations in the basic plan.

## AN APPROACH TO
## THE TEACHING OF BEGINNERS

The following approach is one way of starting folk dance with younger children who have either not danced before or who have done some modern dance and enjoy devising their own dances. It would not be suitable for older girls or for recreational groups because, in all probability, they would prefer to work on traditional dances straight away. Three or four introductory lessons should be sufficient to help dancers to experience some of the simple steps that recur in most folk dances, namely walk, run, skip, gallop, polka and perhaps waltz. The general aim in these first lessons is to give young people the chance to dance with other people, helping them to develop sympathy with the music before imposing the discipline of set dances.

*Specific aims*
1   To improve the resilience of feet and ankles and to demand from the start that the feet are not scraped along the ground but placed as if on a surface like grass. Folk dance was not originally danced on a smooth floor.

2   To encourage the natural use of hands as used in ordinary social behaviour. Shake hand grasp is the normal use although other more complicated holds will later be used.

3 To demand that the body is held naturally and easily when dancing. Good poise is a feature of most folk dances and is more easily encouraged when showing and learning how other people move. A person resisting an unfashionable upright carriage will willingly assume it for an understood purpose. Making this demand in one specific learning situation fosters the sense of poise which later may be adopted generally.

4 To work for a certain containment, which is a feature of most folk dances. The feet are usually kept under the body even when travelling and large leg gestures are rarely used by women and girls. It would of course be unwise to restrict the natural vitality of young dancers so one would not overstress this point. When the pupils become more advanced, they soon learn to save their energy on finding that some dances go on literally for hours. The older dancers often boast that it is the young people who have to drop out first.

5 To help dancers to move naturally with one another, showing concern when turning a partner or when leading her to place. The often heard 'smile to your partner' produces an artificial appearance of enjoyment. Some dances are gay, some are solemn, but the dancers must always be aware of and care for one another when dancing together.

6 To develop the habit of listening to and feeling the rhythm and phrasing of music. Some children and adults find difficulty in keeping time to music even when dancing simple steps. This inability causes embarrassment and is one of the reasons why some adolescents and adults are unwilling to join in social dance. It is important not to draw attention to an arhythmic individual. One of the best answers is to encourage a regular changing of partners so that good dancers can help the less able.

*A sample lesson for beginners*
There is no one correct way to prepare a lesson for beginners, the following plan is given only to show how some of the specific aims may be realised. The three sections are the same as in the basic plan, but the emphasis here is on using the steps freely and on exploring ways of using simple formations.

*Introduction*
1 Dance freely about the room to the music; pick out steps that some have tried and let all share them.

Encourage the dancers to move in all directions and to try to find ways of travelling sideways. It is not enough to ask the dancers to change direction. They must be helped to effect the changes. Two simple suggestions are enough at this stage: one, slow down to anticipate the change; two, alter the tilt of the body slightly to help to change from moving forward to backwards.

2 At the beginning of each musical phrase or sentence change either the step or the direction so that the teacher can see whether the class can hear a musical phrase. She may have to help by asking the dancers to clap at the beginning of every phrase but this should only be necessary with a class which has had no experience of dance or music.

3 Check that all can walk, run, skip, gallop and polka in time with the music. It is helpful to dance the polka forwards, holding hands in twos so that the dancers can help one another.

4 Find out as many ways as possible of dancing with a partner. The teacher should notice unusual ideas and show them so that all may try. She must also be prepared to suggest ways that will be required later in folk dances, eg turning partners with right, left and both hands, dancing back to back, towards and away from each other, one partner chasing the other, and dancing together with a variety of grasps. She must still demand that with all these ideas the musical rhythm and phrasing are followed.

*Practice*
1 Work on simple practices for resilience in feet and ankles. Springs on both feet and one foot can be joined with simple pointing movements of the toes and heels. Each dancer should be encouraged to make up a simple sequence of steps which includes springs and simple leg gestures. The sequence may include a turning movement. It should be practised until it can be repeated exactly as it will be needed later in the dance. On some of the steps, such as the polka, which the class find difficult to pick up and need to practise more slowly, additional work will be required. It will be found necessary to build up performance gradually to the correct tempo.

A simple sequence of steps should then be introduced since this will be useful when traditional dances are later taught. Even in this section with its emphasis on improving movement, there must be a feeling of dance in every practice. Each sequence should be presented as a short dance in its own right.

## Dance
The aim is for each couple to make up a simple dance within a set framework which in this example is the musical form. The music chosen should have clearly defined A and B sections that the class can easily distinguish.

### 1  A  MUSIC
Partners dance together using some of the ideas for travelling learned earlier in the lesson. Sometimes this travelling with a partner can be an entirely spontaneous part of the dance and can vary on every repeat. At other times the teacher may insist that each couple practises its own sequence so that it can be repeated exactly. Above all, the dancers must dance with each other and in sympathy with the music.

### B  MUSIC
One partner dances the sequence of springing steps made up earlier in the lesson while the other partner watches and either accompanies with hand-clapping or tries to copy the step.

### 2  A  MUSIC
Partners again travel together but use very different steps and formations from those in 1 A music.

### B  MUSIC
The other partner now shows her springing step, accompanied or copied by partner. The dance can now be given an entrance and an exit which would mean repeating the A music at the beginning and the end of the dance. When the whole dance has been practised, each half of the class may watch the other half dance. In this way the satisfaction of a simple dance composition is both felt and seen.

## THE TEACHING OF MIXED GROUPS
It is important to teach folk dancing to boys and girls together. If they have already shared in modern dance classes in the primary school, they should readily adapt to mixed folk dancing at the right time in the secondary school. In the primary school boys are not interested in dancing with girls and in any case, folk dance is restricting for young children. The ideal time to start is at adolescence when the boys do want to dance with the girls, but often feel inferior because the girls have continued with dance in the early years of the secondary school, whereas the boys have not. It is this gap that causes a problem, although

it would be a minor one if good modern dance had been taught earlier. The real difficulty is encountered when a large proportion of the boys have done little or no dance at all.

Before starting to dance with the girls, boys should take one or two courses on dance specifically for men. In England, Morris and Sword dances suggest themselves, while in Scotland and Ireland there are many traditional dances for men. Most countries have a good deal of suitable material, and it seems right that boys should approach dance in a masculine way and so avoid the expostulation that it is only for girls. Through such courses, boys gain suitable rhythmical experience and learn to perform co-ordinated movements requiring dexterity and skill. When the time seems ripe, and this will vary in different schools and even for different classes, couple and set dances should be introduced to both sexes. There may be initial difficulties, but once they are solved the groups will study folk dance together as they do other subjects.

At the beginning, the teacher often endeavours to find dances that will appeal to the boys and may neglect the special aptitudes of the girls. Sometimes the boys receive more praise than they know they have really earned, and neither they nor the girls appreciate it. In any case the boys would not have a sense of inferiority, distracting to the class, if they joined the girls with confidence gained in having mastered difficult men's dances. The teacher points out that the dances will now consist of couple, set and chain dances in which sometimes the role of the sexes is not markedly different, but on other occasions, the men will show off their acrobatic feats to the women.

In the past, the problems have been accentuated largely because men have not had as much practice in the teaching of dance as women. In many colleges today this omission is being rectified, particularly in modern dance, although in some colleges folk and country dancing is learnt. As in the schools, the courses in the colleges must be mixed, and both men and women should be equally prepared to teach boys and girls together. Some successful lessons occur today when men and women teachers together take large numbers for social dancing preparatory to the Christmas party.

The advantages of mixed folk dancing are obvious. Boys and girls learn to dance together naturally, the boy showing the courtesy to the girl which every folk dance demands, while the girl enjoys the support that a good male dancer can give her in difficult figures. This type of dance is an excellent preparation for social life with boys and girls dancing together without diffidence and self-consciousness.

The problem is not easy to solve in single sex schools. It is always possible to make suggestions as to ways in which boys' and girls' schools could plan joint activities, but it is not easy to solve the difficulties of distance and time-tables. It should, however, be possible for two neighbouring schools to agree to set aside one afternoon for mixed activities of which folk dance should be one option. After-school clubs are also feasible, but in both these cases the shyest boys and girls, who most need the classes, may not join.

In the girls' schools, dance will probably play a part in the physical education programme, although it is disappointing to discover how often it does not. In many schools, however, both folk and modern dance are well taught. But even with the best of teachers, folk dance for girls alone cannot be ideal. It lacks a second dimension, the needed contrast of the men's strength and virility with the grace and flow of the women's movements. When girls dance as boys, they frequently exaggerate their efforts and it is wise to avoid the couple dance since they tend to make it look too pretty, lacking the earthy quality of dances originally evolved by peasants. There are some attractive dances for women only, but they are mostly in chain formation, and a course based on these dances alone could give a limited conception of folk dance.

In the boys' schools there is usually no dance at all, and this is a serious omission. A fine games player and a good athlete may appear physically illiterate in the dance lesson. Because he thinks that only strong, objective movement is right for boys, he has only learnt certain aspects of physical education. Yet dance is part of physical education in its fullest sense and folk dance in particular helps co-ordination and rhythm, as well as teaching much about different movement styles. It is also socially important for a boy to be able to dance, and it is vitally necessary in boys' schools that dance should be taught and should include some traditional folk dances for men.

Teaching folk dancing is surely the best way to break down the barrier that has arisen in this country against dance for boys. Attitudes are changing and today the time is ripe for dance for everybody. Young people are less self-conscious and inhibited than earlier generations and should take readily to dancing together. They enjoy exciting rhythms, with their own social dances demanding a highly developed sense of rhythm. Folk dance, with its emphasis on the rhythmic beat should particularly help those who find it difficult to join in the dances of their own generation. It would be well for the teacher and club leader to remember this great rhythmic interest when introducing folk dancing to both boys and girls. The dances with exciting rhythm such as those from eastern Europe, Spain and Portugal would have an obvious appeal. There are interesting rhythms to be found in the dances of most countries, and dances with less rhythmic appeal could well be introduced to show contrast.

Many women teachers, experienced in the teaching of folk dancing to girls only, may wonder whether standards would not deteriorate if mixed dancing became the accepted form. Their misgivings would be justified if they had to combine classes of girls, experienced in dance, with boys who had had no preparation. Even if the boys had had some course in men's dances, it would only be fair to point out that the standards would be different. Many of the delightful dances done by girls only would be replaced by a more virile form of dance which might seem less graceful, but would have other qualities which brought it into the realm of true folk dance.

## THE SOCIAL APPROACH

This approach is particularly suitable for all members of recreational groups who have joined the class as a leisure activity. Some of the suggestions might be applicable to school clubs, but they are most suited for adults young and old who want to enjoy folk dance and perhaps join in folk dances when travelling. Enjoyment should be a by-product of all learning situations, but in schools the acquisition of knowledge must surely be the first aim. In recreational classes, on the other hand, the emphasis on enjoyment within a good social atmosphere must be in the forefront of the teacher's thinking. She, too, sets out with the aim of giving of her knowledge, but with a difference in stress.

*Suggested methods*
When depth of knowledge is desired in a recreational class, the usual plan of the lesson would be followed, with the stress on careful step practice and the study of movement characteristics. However, in social clubs in which simpler dances are taught, the steps are better acquired by repetition within the dances themselves and by demonstration by some

good dancers in the group. This was how folk dances were originally picked up in the community. The following suggestions are applicable to the teaching of English, Irish, Scottish, Welsh or European dances.

1 *Demonstration* Select one group to make up a set and teach them the dance while the others look on and see how the dance goes. This is particularly useful for large numbers or small rooms and is used a great deal by the English Folk Dance and Song Society at parties. It is not as useful if many people know the dances and the practice should never be over-used.

2 *Learning by doing* Some people learn best by being swung into a dance even if at first they cause a state of mild confusion. A little laughter can help to ease tension and quickly resolve the situation. In schools, one teaches to avoid mistakes, hence the careful preparation in the lesson plan. With older groups the aim is to let the participants attempt the whole dance, so that as on social occasions, they learn by repeating it as often as possible. It is important for the group to acquire a repertoire so that, in later sessions, known dances can be interspersed with the learning of new work.

3 *Following a caller* As a start to a lesson this method, taken from American square dance, can be applied to the teaching of the simple social dances of almost any country. The caller keeps the dancer moving from figure to figure without stopping to teach, the dancers following the words which are spoken in rhythm. A typical call might be:

'All join hands and circle right,
  keep hold of hands and circle left,
  Into the centre and fall back twice,
  swing your partner and promenade round.'

Some of such simple suggestions might be used to get the class going. The lesson plan is not clearly defined and depends very much on the type and standard of the work being taught. The teacher must ensure that there is a rich diet of good tunes and progressively varied dances in the programme. The word programme is the key to the approach, implying a folk-dance evening rather than a formal lesson.

The teaching of recreational work may be interpreted wrongly as a rather casual process. On the contrary, it must be of a very high standard as adults are critical of poor teaching and enjoy being 'put through it' with firmness, appreciating the knowledge that lies behind.

The facilities in which the classes are held are very important in this type of work. A dreary hall with no comfortable chairs or provisions for refreshments, makes a poor setting for a recreational folk dance evening. Every effort should be made to find the brightest room and one in which coffee can be served during the evening. This allows people to rest and to talk to one another which is part of the attraction of the class. Talking by spectators during the class has to be limited as this lessens the value of the teaching, but the amount allowed would vary with the nature of the class and with the teacher. If it is difficult to find the right kind of social accommodation, small groups can often dance in a large room in a member's house. Many more people will appreciate the social atmosphere of a home and all can take their turn to provide the refreshments. If the room is small everyone will not be able to dance at once. However, they can watch carefully with the challenge that only the first group will be taught the dance and that the others must follow. It is, in fact, one of the methods suggested even if the room is large. Sometimes it might be valuable, if the dances of one country have been studied, to spend a short time looking at slides or a film either of the dances or of something peculiar to the country and its people.

All the suggestions about teaching, method and lesson plan are not nearly as important as is the atmosphere created by the teacher herself. This point will be appreciated by experienced recreational leaders but may not be realised so clearly by those accustomed to teaching students or children. The teacher must learn that the chat with the members of the class, at the beginning and end of the lesson and during coffee, are as important as the planning of the lesson. She must go ready to enjoy herself *with* the class.

## THE TEACHING OF SIMPLE CHAIN DANCES

Many of the circle and chain dances of eastern Europe have a strangely rhythmic interest, with few difficult basic steps or intricate changes of formation. Thus a change in the method of teaching with a less clearly defined lesson plan is suggested.

It is perhaps easier to think of leading rather than teaching some of the simpler dances, in that a careful analysis of individual steps is often not necessary. Such dances are easier to learn if treated as a whole. There has to be teaching, but it is less obvious since it is the subtlety of the apparently easy step that is so difficult to convey. Probably the walking step is the most difficult of all because in the everyday movement individual and racial characteristics show most clearly.

The music is of vital importance in learning these dances and the class should listen carefully until the tune and movement are as one. Sometimes the musical sequence is not strictly followed; so that the sequence, when repeated, does not start at the beginning of the musical phrase. This is difficult for our western ears. In most dances, however, the teacher must know exactly where to start the music if the step is being analysed. In music in which bars of 2/4 follow some of 7/8 the problem is not easy to solve. Singing while dancing often helps the dancers to get the feel of the movement and it is a usual feature of many of the dances. This means that a class must have a good deal of opportunity to listen to records with vocal accompaniment. If words are not available it is better to choose unusual sounds rather than the customary 'la-la' with its associations with a lyrical style. Records with vocal or orchestral accompaniment are better than the best pianist in that they help to transport the teacher and class from the culture of the west to that of the east.

Some of the following suggestions bear some resemblance to those in *The Social Approach* in that the lesson often starts off with a simple dance or with one already known and leads on to a more difficult one without a clearly defined practice section. The methods of approach will vary according to the different type of chain dance which could be divided into: those based on the improvisation on a basic step; and those based on rhythmical sequences.

### Dances based on improvisation by the leader or group

Improvisation is a feature of some dances of the Slavonic and Balkan countries. The dances are built up, usually by the leader of the chain, from walking, closing and crossing steps, runs and step hops. A lesson may, therefore, start with each dancer walking to the music and then trying out variations on these basic steps. Useful suggestions might include varying the timing of the walks, travelling sideways crossing one foot first in front and then behind the other, using the closing step as a means of changing direction and of varying the tension so that it may be a clicking step or a soft sitting step. Each dancer then makes up a sequence and practises it until it can be repeated exactly. The class then divides into short chains with a leader (each person taking a turn) and a tail dancer (always a man at both ends of a mixed group). The chain must then follow the leader's every move and later, with the permission of the leader, the tail may be allowed to lead.

The danger of this approach is obvious. The characteristic style of the particular region may well be lost as each individual has so much freedom and so little experience on which to build. A knowledgeable teacher can help to induce the style during the practice of the basic steps largely through dancing with the group. If in the locality there is a dancer from the particular area willing to come and give one lesson so that all can see and feel the type of movement, then the class should be able to build on the basic steps as suggested. In the future, it is hoped that more films and film loops may become available. (Meanwhile it is sometimes possible to borrow films from embassies.)

If the teacher is uncertain of giving the freedom of improvisation, then it is wiser to start the lesson by setting a simple, well-known dance. Put on the record, join hands in a circle and dance the dance again and again until all can perform it. An inner circle of confident dancers helps those in the outer circle to follow more easily, so that they do not have to concentrate on watching the teacher who, being on the opposite side of the circle, may confuse those who try to mirror her movements.

The lesson builds up to include a more difficult dance, which the teacher or local leader has set. It may be necessary to practise some of the steps and variations of this separately before starting the dance itself. Whenever possible, too much analysis should be avoided. The dances to be taught in schools and in clubs should be simple and fairly short and should be danced when possible as wholes or as themes and variations in this particular type of chain dance.

### Dances based on rhythmic sequences

Many chain dances are composed of rhythmic sequences of varying lengths and are much more set than the dances based mainly on the improvisation on a basic step. It is often necessary to divide the dance into two or more parts, joining each as it is learnt. Some of the longer chain dances need, not so much analysis, as careful division of the rhythmical sequences. It is not quite the same as teaching the steps and figures of a western European dance with set steps which must be learnt separately.

Some dancers like to see the whole dance once through before learning the parts. For this reason the longer dances need to be approached by showing the group how the dance is composed of several sequences which are then repeated. Sometimes each sequence is repeated a set number of times while at other times it is only danced once. The teacher has to ensure that she can not only dance the whole dance, but also dance one of the parts and repeat it until it has been learnt. This is more difficult than it appears and needs practice. The division into parts should be chosen because the sections belong together rhythmically and so can be remembered. Joins must be taught, but analysis, beat by beat, seems endless and illogical in a type of dance so dependent on its rhythmical composition.

## The teaching of steps

### General points

Three factors are of vital importance when teaching a difficult step:

The ability to demonstrate well
The power to use the voice rhythmically and qualitatively
The ability to see the difficulties.

These talents can be used to full advantage only if the teacher has a clear knowledge of what she is trying to teach; knowledge not only of the accurate spatial pattern in the correct rhythm, but the knowledge of the quality of movement and of the particular poise and tension of the body which gives the characteristic style.

Learning by demonstration is the most usual way of picking up the pattern, rhythm and quality of a step. A good demonstration will convey all three aspects of the movement and the quick learner may assimilate them all at once. The average student usually tries to get the feet in the right position at the right time and only later is able to appreciate the more subtle aspects of the step; whether there is any sudden or sustained movement within the step; whether great or little body tension is required; the degree of resilience or hardness within a step. It is usual, although sometimes dangerous, to over-emphasise any of these

qualities in order to drive a point home. If this is done then the step must be finally shown as it should be danced and the class must be allowed to dance it again after the accurate demonstration. It is sometimes necessary to demonstrate a common fault and even advisable to let the class make the mistake and then immediately correct it to feel the difference in the quality of the action. This method of teaching by contrast is useful as long as the corrected step is repeated again and again in order to establish it. Good demonstration is the quickest and surest way to achieve results, but the other two factors are also important.

A teacher can help the class to learn the rhythm and quality of a step by using her voice to emphasise these two aspects. The voice can also direct where the feet should be placed by words used descriptively and still rhythmically, eg

$$1 \qquad 2 \qquad 1 \qquad 2 \qquad 1 \quad \text{and} \qquad 2$$
'step behind, step in front, step, stamp, stamp'.

When the teacher speaks in the rhythm of the music the non-musical student, who does not seem to hear the musical beat, is especially helped. In some dances, particularly those of certain eastern countries, the step is danced through the musical phrase so that a particular step is not always danced to the same bars of the music. The use of actual directions, spoken in rhythm, helps a class to learn not to follow the musical phrase but to dance through it. As well as helping rhythm and direction the voice can convey *how* the step should be danced. When a sudden closing of the feet is needed, the sharp and incisive use of voice will help to produce this sharp action. Equally the voice can suggest a relaxed, leisurely movement requiring a giving into the ground. It can also control the actual timing of such a step which is often slow and sustained. Very often the teacher is dancing with the class and using her voice at the same time; she may then stop dancing and continue to use her voice so that she can observe more easily while still helping the class.

Good observation is probably one of the essentials of the good teacher. If a teacher of folk dance can see the difficulties of the individual in particular and of the class in general and has a clear image of how the step should be danced, she will find ways to good results. An experienced teacher is aware of what difficulties to expect and will know what points to give. The less experienced teacher needs to think of what is likely to be difficult when preparing the lesson.

Often the older teacher will make up for her inability to demonstrate as well as she would wish with good observation and use of voice. The voice can give the dynamism which her demonstration may lack and she will be able to select a member of the class to demonstrate who has the very quality needed. This ability to pick out the different members to show certain points well is of value and is enjoyed by the class as they realise that the work is within their scope and that their efforts are noticed and appreciated.

These three important factors do not come without practice. Some of this practice can be done when preparing the lesson. Too often a dance lesson is prepared in a sitting position and in silence. The preparation of a folk dance lesson must be active with the voice singing the tune and practising coaching in rhythm.

*Stages in the teaching of a step*
There are three possible stages in the teaching of a step, although the methods vary considerably according to the type of step.

1 Demonstration   2 Analysis and development
3 Observation and improvement

The easier steps will be taught first and may only need a good demonstration and practice. The more difficult steps, taught later in the lesson, will probably need all three stages of teaching in order to achieve good results.

*Demonstration*
For all steps the class must be placed so that all can see the demonstration which must be as good as the teacher can make it. Where she places herself and the class varies between travelling steps and steps on the spot, so suggestions for both are given. Each teacher will naturally find her own best methods or adapt some of these to suit the special needs of her class.

*Travelling steps*   The teacher demonstrates in the centre of an informal circle, all the dancers facing the same way, ready to follow on immediately after seeing the demonstration. The teacher dances for 8 bars, using her feet and voice to emphasise the point. Without stopping the music, the dancers copy the step, also dancing for 8 bars. This can be repeated until the rhythm and pattern are firmly established. A new step is then shown and repeated as before. If the two steps are part of the same dance sequence then they must be practised in the same form as in the dance,

eg after teaching polka and step hop the sequence 2 polkas, 4 step hops, 1 polka, 2 step hops, 1 polka, 2 step hops must be practised. Sometimes difficult travelling steps are more easily taught using the length of the room, all facing the same way as the teacher.

Since it involves plenty of movement and the minimum of standing still and listening this DO-DANCE method is often used at the start of the lesson with simple travelling steps.

*Steps on the spot*   The class should be well spaced and all facing the teacher. She should either show the step facing the class, in which case she must start with the foot opposite that required by the class, or dance with her back to the class. A good plan is to demonstrate facing the class; then turn and dance with the girls as they copy; turn again to face the class to note progress. This involves two changes of feet on the part of the teacher so that she always moves in the same direction as the class. With a large number of dancers and a difficult step, it is often advisable to repeat this sequence facing the class from each side of the room in turn. This ensures that everyone can see the teacher's step and she can see each member of the class, not only those at the front.

The same principle of DO-DANCE is followed with the music and voice supplementing visual learning. The majority will now have picked up the step but will need help with detail while a few need to have the step broken down before they can learn it at all.

*Analysis and development*
An inexperienced teacher must prepare this stage of breaking down the step and building it up very carefully as poor analysis can cause dancers to lose a step which they had acquired from the demonstration. The difficulty often lies in the poor build-up of the step after it has been taught in slow motion.

*Stages*   Facing the class the teacher walks through the step with the class very slowly, using her voice to explain what the feet are doing. It must be made clear where the step begins and ends. If balance is difficult, the step can start on the flat of the foot and gradually increase in speed on the balls of the feet, introducing a springing action if and when required. The holding of hands also helps balance as well as allowing a better dancer to help a slower learner.

This is a time for individual correction as a step wrongly learnt is difficult to re-teach. At the end of the analysis the rhythm is gradually brought in without any pause in the movement until it is nearly up to time; at this juncture the accompanist can join in. If records or tapes are being used it is vital first to bring the step up to the speed of the recorded sound. This means that the teacher must know the exact speed herself. Otherwise, she will have difficulty in fitting the step to the music. This needs a good deal of practice in listening so that the voice can gradually be used rhythmically and at the required speed without any musical aid.

A complicated step should be divided into learnable sections; the first part must be taught and then the second before the join is practised. The two parts must then be danced together until they follow one another naturally.

Once a step is learnt in its simplest form it should be practised in all the ways in which it is to be used in the dance, turning, advancing and retiring, with a partner and using the required holds.

To summarise, the more preparation put into the practices and sequences the less interruption will there be in the actual teaching of the dance itself.

*Observation and improvement*
Obviously both observation and correction have been going on throughout the earlier stages and it is not always necessary to think of them as a separate section. Sometimes, however, a teacher has been so busy dancing with the class that it is good to ensure that the dancers can do the steps without her help. The opportunity should be taken to stand back and see what she has or has not taught. It is essential to devise some simple method which keeps the class dancing in smaller groups so that individual observation is made easier for the teacher. The following are a few suggestions which may be useful to ensure that what has been taught has been carefully observed. Travelling steps and steps on the spot are dealt with separately as they demand different methods.

*Travelling steps*     a  Lines advance up the room, each dancing for 8 bars before the next line starts. When the first line reaches the front, members slip unobtrusively to the back ready to start again. It is always better to speak in terms of musical bars than in terms of numbers of steps as the attention of the class is then directed to listening carefully to the music. This is an essential in learning to dance.

b  Instead of advancing in lines up the room, the class can travel across the diagonal from each of the back corners, holding hands in twos or threes, a couple or trio coming alternatively from each corner. To avoid meeting in the middle one corner starts 8 bars ahead of the other. It is a good formation for a step that demands a sense of travel and the dancers enjoy the greater length of space in which to dance.

These two simple procedures enable the teacher to see individuals more clearly in an organised situation.

*Steps on the spot*     The checking up here may simply demand that the teacher stands back and really looks at her class. She can have a longer look if she asks one half of the class to dance, the other half to follow after a set number of bars. It may be the time to teach some of the longer sequences required in the dance. The teacher then has time to watch some continuous dancing. She may realise that although most of the dancers have acquired the correct step patterns, they have not yet learnt the delicacy or the strength of movement needed. Sometimes it is enough just to give a reminder or a demonstration but on other occasions when it is necessary to go on with the work, note the weakness and decide what to work on during the next lesson.

Pupil observation is often used in the teaching of steps. It can be useful if, and only if, the dancers know exactly what to look for. A younger girl is only able to notice the positions of the lines and whether her partner's foot is extended or whether she is stepping in front instead of behind. Older girls who have the same teacher for modern dance can observe not only positioning of the feet but also the quality in movement. Sometimes a class is asked to choose the best movement. This is only satisfactory if the teacher and class have established a clear understanding that the ability to select is a proof of knowledge. The obvious danger is that the same dancers are usually chosen. This practice should be used sparingly except with students or leaders. The teacher herself can often find a poor dancer who has got a particular quality that is needed such as resilience or heaviness. By selecting her to show this point the girl will gain confidence, one of the most essential needs for learning dance or indeed any subject.

The learning of a step can be the dullest part of a lesson or it can give a great sense of achievement. It all depends on the teacher. Some have natural attributes for this type of teaching but careful preparation is probably the greatest single road to success and can avoid unnecessary time being spent on this part of the lesson.

# Some particular steps

| | |
|---|---|
| Hop on L lifting R forward | *u* |
| Step forward on R | I |
| Close L to R | *and* |
| Step forward on R | 2 |
| Repeat starting with L | *u* I *and* 2 |

*Teaching points*

I When danced without a hop the step is danced either slightly on the ball of the foot and the supporting knees slightly bend (Czech) or on whole foot with easy knees (Austrian).

2 When danced with a hop the step is danced on the ball of the foot, the height varying with the country, but there is a lifted appearance cause by the raised leg which should lift the whole body on the hop.

*Description of step*
Backwards—with a hop. As in the forward step except that the free foot, instead of being lifted forwards is neatly placed behind the supporting ankle on the hop.

*Teaching point*

I It is a help to dance this step preceded by the forward step so that the rhythm is established. eg

8 polkas forward, 8 backward,
4 polkas forward, 4 backward,
4 polkas forward, 4 backward

The finer point of where the lifted foot should go can then be added. The point about 'no scraping' should be particularly noted here. Since it is difficult to travel far backwards, the step should be kept short when danced forwards.

*Description of step*
SIDEWAYS—WITH A HOP

| | |
|---|---|
| Hop on L picking R up behind ankle | *u* |
| Step sideways on R | I |
| Close L to R (often instep to heel) | *and* |
| Step sideways on R | 2 |
| Repeat with hop on R travelling to left | *u* I *and* 2 |

## POLKA

The term polka is used freely in folk dance but the step differs in style according to the country and should not be thought of as a step with a standard pattern but as a step with the rhythm of *u*, I, *and*, 2 in which the feet do

*u*   I   *and*   2   *u*   I   *and*   2
hop  right, close, right; hop, left, close, left

The step itself varies from the Czech polka without a hop, to the Victorian polka with the picked up foot, a ballroom version which has influenced the folk dance step in many countries. In Britain the step has great differences when danced by the English, the Irish or the Scots, the latter two calling it the *promenade step* and *skip change of step* respectively. A basic version of the step is described here and should be used in connection with *Approach to beginners*. The step can be danced forwards, backwards, sideways and turning and these variations are described accompanied by some points for teaching.

*Description of step*

FORWARDS—WITHOUT A HOP

| | |
|---|---|
| Step forwards on R | I |
| Close L to R | *and* |
| Step forward on R | 2 |
| Repeat starting with L | I *and* 2 |

Note   *u* = $\frac{1}{4}$ beat
   *and* = $\frac{1}{2}$ beat   *(see page 33 for abbreviations)*

1 Emphasise the start with a quick hop and the picked up foot.

2 Short steps on balls of feet with very little travelling.

3 Ensure change of weight on the close.

4 Once the step is established, introduce the turn both to the right and to the left.

*Note* The sideways step is the basis of the polka turn although the method used in *Approach to beginners* is based on the turn on the gallop step as does the description of polka turn here.

5 The step is resilient, often light in quality, especially when danced high on the balls of the feet. When the whole foot is used, the step is heavier but still has a buoyant quality.

*Description of step*
*Polka turning* This step consists of two polka sideways steps, danced with a partner, using half a turn to the right on each polka. The following quick method of teaching the turn for social purposes or for beginners is based on the gallop step and produces very easily the type of simple step used as the turning polka in many countries.

*Teaching points*
1 All face the side of the room and dance the following sequence, first alone, then with a partner using waltz or waist and shoulder grasp.

   8 gallop steps to the right, 8 to the left,
   4 gallop steps to the right, 4 to the left,
   2 to right, 2 to left, 2 to right, 2 to left

2 Develop the 2 gallop sequence with half a turn on every second step: Gallop and turn, gallop and turn always to the right, so that a whole turn is completed after the two movements. This sequence should be danced up the length of the room, first alone and then with a partner. Couples start sideways to the line of dance, holding a firm grasp so that the amount of turn is minimal. They are then dancing a simple polka step, although the rhythm of the teacher's voice needs to help the change from the even gallop to the uneven polka, eg gallop and turn changes to hop, step, close step. The class usually effects this change naturally if a polka tune is used for the practice.

## WALTZ
The fact that the waltz step is danced in 3/4 time seems to set up an immediate barrier for some children and adults. The following suggestions may be helpful.

1 *Walking* Without stressing any change of musical time, take it for granted that the class can walk to every musical beat. Gradually the pianist accents, or, if a record is being used, the teacher claps the first beat of each bar. The teacher and dancers follow this without too much attention being paid to a stamping action on the first beat.

2 *Rise and fall* Using the whole foot on the first step and the balls of the feet on steps 2 and 3, the teacher dances the flowing waltz step saying 'down, up, up' as the class follows her. The step is then danced forwards and backwards until the dancers become fully conversant with the feel of the step. The teacher must realise that one waltz step is danced to each bar of music.

3 *Balance* After the travelling stage in which the feet have not been joined, a balance from side to side and forwards and backwards can be practised as a rest from travelling. No attention is drawn to the closing of the feet although this is bound to happen. When too much thought is given to the join, some dancers do not know on which foot their weight is when the feet are together and so are uncertain on which foot to step.

4 *Joining* Later, but not too soon, a class should be able to produce variations on the travelling step by sometimes joining the feet on the third step, 'step, step, close'; then they try closing on the second step, 'step, close, step', although this is not so often used as the passing step and the closing on the third step. The important point for the teacher to stress, is that the weight of the body is transferred on each of the three beats. This apparently casual approach may prevent the student being too aware of what to do with his or her feet.

*Waltz turning*
A class should have mastered the rise and fall in waltz rhythm before attempting waltz turning with a partner. There is no quick method of teaching this step as there is for the polka, and repeated practice is needed before a whole class can waltz easily. When analysed, the step consists of one forward waltz step turning followed by one sideways waltz step turning. This is the woman's step; the man does the reverse, ie

one sideways step turning followed by one forward waltz step turning.

*Description of step*
Couples stand sideways to the line of dance (men with back to centre of room) holding ballroom or hip and shoulder grasp. It is easier to complete the full turn with ballroom grasp as the dancers are closer together and so do not have so far to turn.

*Ballroom grasp*   The man has his right arm round the woman's waist; her left arm rests on his shoulder; the other hands are grasped and arms held horizontal and straight pointing along the line of dance.

Beat 1   The man steps round his partner with a sideways step on his left foot while she steps forward between his feet with her right foot using a heel lead.

Beat 2   Still turning, the man steps sideways almost on the spot with his right foot while the woman takes a small step, almost sideways, on her left foot.

Beat 3   The half turn is completed when the man closes up with his left foot, changing weight, and the woman does the same with her right foot.

The step is now repeated, the man going through between the woman's feet on his right foot while she goes round him on her left foot. At the end of this second waltz step one complete turn has been made.

*Teaching points*
1  *Balance of weight*   The woman leans back slightly away from her partner to balance the partner's weight and so help the momentum of the turn. Before starting to dance, the man may be asked to let go of his partner; she should then lose balance if she is really leaning back.

2  *Rise and fall*   This is danced as in the travelling step, 'down, up, up'. The step should be smooth without too much accent on the first step or with an exaggerated or sudden rise and fall.

3  *Flow*   This is the chief characteristic of the step and it is important to work for it in the preliminary practices of the travelling step. Otherwise, it will not be easy to achieve it in the turning step.

4  *Lines*   It is a help to practise the turn up the room to ensure that the path is straight, ie 2 complete waltz steps to one whole turn. The couples usually tend to over-turn and can check up more easily by facing a different side wall after each waltz step. The step must finally be practised in a circle, where it will probably be used in the dance.

## TWO-STEP
Having learnt to turn with a partner, using 3 steps as in a waltz turn, it is sometimes necessary to complete a whole turn in two steps.

*Description of step*
The couples stand sideways to the line of dance using any of the usual waltz holds. The step is similar to the waltz in that the couples revolve round each other while progressing round the room with a walking step. To a lesser degree than in the waltz, the dancers place their feet alternately through and round each other's feet, but the main means of turn is a pivot on the supporting foot as well as on the stepping foot. The step has no rise and fall and is danced on rather straight but not stiff legs. Sometimes it is danced on the balls of the feet but at other times almost on the whole foot. The rhythm is straight 2/4.

*Teaching points*
This step requires skill and needs a lot of practice with a partner so that the two seem to dance as one.
1  Practise dancing across the room in couples, either on a marked line or towards a fixed object in order to maintain a straight line. To prevent giddiness and to help the dancers to analyse the amount of turn completed in two steps (one two-step), not more than 8 steps should be practised at one time. Dancers should lean away from one another in order to help momentum. A close hold is also helpful.

2  The man should turn his head towards the line of dance at the start of each new turn. In the polka the head is turned at each half turn.

3  Couples, having practised the step across the room, must now move round the room as in the dance. They must still retain the right amount of turn and stay in the line of dance. It is unwise to revolve more often in practice than is required in the dance.

## SETTING STEP

This step, often danced with a partner, is a *pas-de-basque*, and may be danced on the spot, turning, travelling forwards and backwards.

*Description of step*

In essence this step consists of three changes of weight:

| | |
|---|---|
| Spring on to R, | 1 |
| Close L to R, with the heel of L to | |
| instep of R changing weight, | *and* |
| Change weight to R, keeping it behind L | 2 |

The step is resilient and often danced on the balls of the feet. In some countries the feet are turned out and extended (Scotland), but usually these features are not exaggerated. There is also a difference in the men's and women's step in certain countries, the men raising the knees and springing high on the first step. This variation is usually found when the step is danced in 3/4 time instead of the more usual 2/4 or 6/8 when the step is smaller and lighter. Again there may sometimes be very little placement of the feet, one in front of the other as described, so that the step almost becomes a balance with the feet side by side (England).

*Stages of teaching*

1 Walk the rhythm; step, change, weight, on the whole foot to ensure that the weight is changed on each step or beat. Repeat on alternate feet until the rhythm is learnt.

*Note* In 2/4 time the rhythm is uneven, 1 *and* 2; in 3/4 time the rhythm is even, 1, 2, 3.

2 Continue to dance the rhythm on the balls of the feet.

3 Spring on to the first step with a resilient change of weight on the next two beats. The usual mistake is to omit the change of weight on the second count.

4 Add, if necessary, the correct foot placement or any variation according to the particular dance style.

5 Build a sequence of 4 steps on the spot, followed by 4 turning, making sure that the weight change and foot placement (if important) does not change on the turn.

6 Practise advancing and retiring. The forward steps have to be fairly short in order to accommodate them to the backward steps in which travel is difficult.

7 Practise setting and turning or any other sequence that is going to be needed in the particular dance.

## PIVOT STEP

This is essentially a turning step and can be danced singly, with a partner, or in a basket formation. A step with a somewhat similar rhythm and action, danced sideways or forwards is usually described as a dotting or lame step. Although the pivot step looks simple it is difficult to teach. The following method is usually successful with beginners, although unnecessarily laborious with a good class of students or recreational leaders.

*Description of step*

TURNING TO THE RIGHT

| | |
|---|---|
| Step on R, well turned out, preparing to turn the body to the right | 1 |
| Placing the L on the ball of the foot behind the R, push off so that it takes the weight momentarily, thus allowing the right heel to move round to the right | *u* |
| Replace the whole of weight on the R, still turned out | 2 |
| Repeat the push off with the L | *u* |

Repeat this sequence until the end of the phrase or until the required number of steps have been danced.

TURNING TO THE LEFT

As above, using the L to take the weight on the main beat, pushing off with the R on the *u* beat.

*Teaching points*

1 Facing forwards, establish the sequence of dropping on to the R on every beat with the minimum transfer of weight on the L on the *u* beat. Do not allow any rocking action but get the feeling of the weight being on the forward foot. No turn is made.

2 The receiving knee and ankle should give when they receive the weight. When the rhythm is established the turn to the right should begin, helped by the head and shoulders which really lead into the turn.

*Note* R in front to turn to right. Practise the same turn to the left with the L in front.

3 Practise 8 pivots to the right followed by 8 pivots to the left. This may come naturally but sometimes the class has to be told that there is no transfer of weight on the *u* after the 8th step and that the L must be ready to step forward to start the turn to the left. The body action must slow down at the end of the phrase so that the shoulders are square to the front before the change of direction is made.

# PART THREE

## The Dances

The aim in selecting twelve dances for the third section is to illustrate the principles which have been formulated in the earlier chapters. All the dances have been noted from the dancing of men and women of the country, and after discussion with experts whose names are gratefully recorded in the list of acknowledgments. Nearly all the dances and their steps have been filmed, and it has therefore been possible to return to a visual record to ensure accuracy of detail. Despite this, since variations are common in folk dance, even between one village and the next, readers visiting the countries may well come upon different versions.

Selection has presented a particularly difficult problem since the variety and number of the dances in each country make it impossible to cover even the main types of dance. The choice has been determined chiefly by the wish to emphasise contrast. Those dances have been selected which, through steps, ground pattern, and rhythms, best illustrate the diversity of dancing in the region.

The dances chosen present a wide variety of style and formation. The style of the Breton dances has been strongly affected by the court dance of the Middle Ages, and these dances are the most contained, despite the sprightliness with which they are danced. The Austrian dances in contrast have retained more the atmosphere of the nineteenth century and the dance of the ballroom, with stress on smoothness, flow and turning. Greek dances are rooted in antiquity with some elements almost unchanged to this day. In contrast, the Israeli dance, even though the choreographers have looked to Jewish dances of the past, is very much of the modern world, with drive and a pulsating rhythm.

The same type of comparison can be made between the formations and ground patterns which are characteristic of the countries. In Greece chain dances predominate, and couple dances are rare except in Cyprus, and in the Ionian Islands where Western influence has been felt. Dancing with a partner has little significance in Greece where couple dances are usually antikristos, that is with dancers facing each other. In the Greek chain, though sometimes the dancers are placed alternately man and woman, it is common for a man to lead a line of women, or for the front part of the chain to be of men while the women dance at the end; frequently men and women dance in separate chains. The chain and circle dances in every country are those of the most ancient origin and with deepest ritual significance. Many of the dances of Brittany are chain dances and again in some cases there are separate men's and women's chains. There are couple dances as well and also figure dances in which ground pattern and formations give much of the attraction to the dance. It is in Austria that the figure dance reaches real heights of invention and ingenuity, with unbelievable intertwinings which delight the spectator and bring immense satisfaction to the dancers, whose skill makes it possible for them to master the intricacies and to make all seem easy and natural. The more social Austrian dances are nearly all couple dances, with occasionally one in which the man dances with two girls. Their formation dances are in fact also basically partner dances in which the path of the couple as they dance is woven with that of the other couples in the circle.

A factor which has been important in the selection of the dances has been the need to illustrate the wide range of rhythm and harmony in the dance music, not only between the countries, but also within each country. That the music affects the dance style is apparent even from a study of the limited number of dances in this book. The use that the dancers make of their folk instruments, of their own singing or of sung accompaniment, of the clapping of hands or the stamping of feet, heightens the character of their traditional dance.

If the learner dancers listen to a good recording of typical music from each of these four countries, they will immediately appreciate that the dance styles similarly will be different, even if ground patterns and steps seem sometimes to be alike. Although it may be intended to learn the dances of only one of the countries, there is value in listening to the contrasting music of another country. It is worthwhile, too, to listen to, and perhaps learn, folk songs as well as dance tunes. Great care should be taken to find recordings in which the music is played on traditional instruments.

The piano is not a helpful instrument for accompanying any of these dances, though the teacher may find it useful in the early stages of step practice. The accompanist may be able to play another instrument or help the dancers to sing the tune. Some of the dancers may like to learn to play some of the traditional instruments with guidance from a music colleague. Such an extension of folk dancing seems natural when the dances are seen as part of a wider study. In Brittany, Greece and Israel it is usual for the dancers to sing; the learner more quickly appreciates the relationship of music to movement if he hums or sings as he dances.

John Martin in *The Dance* writes, 'In his beginnings the dancer inevitably sings as he dances . . . When, however, his movements become too strenuous and demand too much breath for him to continue his song, the bystanders take up the singing for him. In time the melodic line of the voice is transferred to an instrument, and since it can play higher and lower than he could possibly sing, it serves even to increase his range of expression. Similarly the rhythmic beating of his feet on the ground is accentuated, and intensified past what he could do himself, by the clapping of hands, the shaking of rattles and the beating of drums . . . if it is really dance music it still retains the rhythmic pulse of his body and the melodic line of his voice; it is, indeed, potentially the dancer's own song'[1].

Recordings provide a poor substitute for live music, but are far superior to music played on unsuitable instruments, which frustrates the dancers' efforts to become steeped in the style of the dance. Records are obtainable in all the countries whose dances are included here; these are undoubtedly better than other records of traditional music, but considerable delay must be expected in getting records from abroad.

To be helpful to the learners, the teacher must know the music really well and be able to recognise and sing every section of the tune; she must be able to explain unusual features in the music of the four countries.

It is especially important to ensure that steps and figures are always accompanied by the correct section of the music, so that, for the dancers, sound and action are closely interwoven. In learning the figure dances, *Treffner Tanz* and the *Jabadao*, the dancers will be able to learn one or two of the figures and to enjoy them as an interim dance if they sing their own accompaniment. In this way they can achieve good standards and get the feel of the dance before proceeding to the complete sequence. Otherwise memorizing will become so demanding that all the character of the dance may be lost.

There is no doubt that one of the features which makes folk dance attractive is the wearing of traditional dress; but the wearing of costume is much more than a means of adding colour and gaiety. Just as it is vital to learn about the style of a dance through its music, so it is essential to understand the effect of the traditional dress on the performance of the dance. To turn the pages of a book of national costume is to understand at once that those who dress so differently will, inevitably, also dance differently. Although the term national costume perhaps conjures up the idea of dressing up, those who have seen the pride with which traditional costume is worn at dance festivals will never make this mistake. Many of the costumes have been in the dancers' families for years, carefully preserved for special occasions. It is not so much the beautiful detail and decoration that our own dancers need to study in order to dance in the correct style; rather, an understanding of shape and weight and texture is required, and the imagination to realise the effect that these will have on the mode of moving. It is useless to try to dance barefoot any but the dances of Israel; the character of many of the Austrian dances has been influenced by the heavy leather shoes of the men. The elaborate head-dresses worn by the Breton women ensure an upright and elegant poise of head and body even in the most lively of the dances. To make and dance with an appropriate head-dress will help our dancers to an understanding of the limitations which it imposes. The leotards worn by many dance groups give no sense of the weight and restriction of the homespun woollen dresses of the women of Macedonia, or of the heavy kilted skirts of their menfolk. It is worth persuading dancers to dress in a way which will make it easier for them to get the feeling of the movement. Some full-gathered, calf-length skirts which the women may borrow will help them to appreciate the need for small steps in the Greek dances and to sense and enjoy the swirl of the skirt in the Austrian waltz and two-step.

It has been possible to include in this volume only one photograph of costume for each country, but teachers and dancers will collect many more from the tourist agency or while on holiday. It is necessary to distinguish between real photographs of men and women in traditional dress and the sometimes very attractive greetings cards whose pictures give a general idea of the costume, but do not otherwise provide accurate information. It is sad that the rapid growth of the tourist trade has led in nearly all these countries to a deterioration in the standard of production of national dolls. They are frequently dressed in most atypical materials so that their garments give the impression of being fancy dress and not genuine clothes worn by real people. When young people bring mementoes of their holidays (and the countries considered in this book are among the most popular for vacations) it is important to help them to distinguish between authentic features and those which are designed merely to catch the eye of the tourist.

From appreciation of the beauty of the costumes the dancers are readily led to further enquiry about the nation, realising that people who differ so much in their dance and costume will also have differing folk customs, and, even in the modern world, different ways of life. Folk dance can thus be used to introduce a vivid picture of the life of another nation, its music, its art and its costume, its language, its customs and its legends. To compare the fairy tales and folk legends which are told in each of the four countries and to perceive links between them and the dances is illuminating. The teacher must be well informed and ready to encourage wide-ranging questions and to help the dancers to find out as much as possible about the background to the dances.

The study of folk lore is complex but a little insight is valuable in enabling dancers to realise that the dances have a meaning and a history and are more than a series of steps and figures. For some this awakening of interest may lead to a much more comprehensive study of folk dance and song.

The countries represented in this book have no political boundaries in common; however the dances selected do show the various types of influence which the dances of one country have upon those of another.

Israel, with the newest of the dances, reveals influences from both East and West. Her dances have been influenced by all the nations whose people have emigrated to form the present state of Israel. Thus the dances owe much to returning Jewish minority groups, and their fluent and untrammelled style also shows the influence of the modern dance of the USA. In return the Israeli dances have been particularly popular in the United States; they may well warrant the title international, so quickly have they spread round the world.

Certainly, apart from those of Israel, none of the dances can be called national, with the exception of those Austrian dances which a group of dancers has suggested should be shared on a nation-wide basis, or those which like the Kalamatianos of Greece have, through general popularity, come to be danced in every part of the land.

More often the dances are shared by several countries. The dances of Macedonian Greece are known and danced in neighbouring Yugoslavia and Bulgaria. Austria, so centrally situated, has social dances which are shared, not only by other German speaking peoples, but, with the whole of Western Europe. In Klagenfurt the dance commonly accepted in Britain as Swedish, *Varsovienne* was included as an Austrian dance and the significance of *vienne* became apparent to the writer; more recently another dancer has claimed that this same dance is Polish by reason of the *Varso* or Warsaw. There is also a French version which may explain the French flavour of the name. It is plain that present political frontiers by no means form the dance boundaries.

In 1895 Lilly Grove wrote, 'To trace a dance from one land to another will often illustrate the historical connection of different peoples; we shall also find the same dances practised by kindred nations, proving that race is a close bond of union between countries geographically distant'[2]. At least one of the Greek dances, *tsakonikos*, was brought to mainland Greece by sea and the dances of the Ionian Islands show marked Italian influence in style and music. It is thought that the Bretons also added to their dances elements brought home by their sea-faring men.

In choosing dances to represent the countries a different type of selection has emerged in each case. The dances of Israel would be known by dancers in every part of the country. To represent France the province of Brittany was chosen and though the dances are widely known they would be danced in differing versions from one locality to another. In like manner the Austrian dances are really represented by the province of Carinthia, though two of them would be known everywhere in Austria. The practice of each of the Greek dances is confined to small local districts and even to villages, and one of them, the Easter *trata* is danced on only one day of the year.

Additionally, some practical issues have been considered in the selection of the dances.

As far as possible dances have been chosen which are not already well-known in Britain. Visiting dancers are reasonably likely to see them when on holiday. Since the intention is to give help at an elementary level, the dances are mostly simple and depend for their success on style and character, rather than on intricate footwork. Where possible dances have been included for which recorded music is available, though the purchase of foreign records in Britain is by no means easy.

The dances are social dances and so represent only a small part of each country's dance resources, since every country has also many ritual dances and dances for special occasions which are quite beyond the scope of the present book.

There is however in all the dances something of the inwardness which tells of the ritual in which they are rooted. As John Martin expressed it the dances are 'for the emotional release of the dancer and without regard for the possible interest of the spectator'[3]. Watching the vast assembly in Klagenfurt, observing at rehearsals in Athens, joining in the dances in Brittany and in Israel, even at the festivals which are in part a commercial venture, there was no doubt that these are dances of the folk. The audience may look, may be drawn by the dancers' absorption into sharing, but the dance goes on regardless. Even in the theatre, the Greek dancers remain focused, apparently oblivious of the audience, as they give themselves up to the music and the spirit of the dance.

The problem is to engender some of this spirit in the teaching of folk dance. Lucille Armstrong, adjudicating at Llangollen has said that the essentials are authenticity of style and tradition, correct performance of steps and figures, continuity of movement, and correct music played in correct style on the correct instruments. She was speaking to dancers presenting the dances of their own nations, but it is towards these goals that we must reach in interesting young people in the dances of other nations.

It is difficult, indeed it is not possible, to transmit all these essentials in the written word and to describe adequately the form and the spirit of the dances, but every effort has been made to present the twelve dances with accuracy.

The very limitations of the book may prove to be a strength if they make dancers wish to go themselves to find more. The chance to join a Breton dance on the beach by the light of car head lamps; or to watch the recreational dance evening of a Young Farmers' Club in Austria; to dance at a wine festival in Greece and then see some of the same dances presented in traditional costume in an open air theatre; to share a day of dance with young Israelis and so to understand their determination even by forcing an entry, to attend a demonstration designed to trace the development of the dances of their new nation. These experiences make the dances real and living. Only when every opportunity is taken by teacher and by dancers to extend their interest in the people and their way of life is the true educational value of folk dance realised.

*References*
[1] John Martin, *The Dance*, Tudor Publishing Co, New York, 1946, pages 14–15
[2] Lilly Grove, FRGS, *Dancing*, Badminton Library, Longmans, Green and Co, 1895, page 8
[3] John Martin, *The Dance*, page 18

*Bibliography*
*World History of the Dance*, Curt Sachs, Norton and Co, New York, 1937
*A History of Dancing*, G Vuiller, Heinemann, London, 1898
*Dancing*, Lilly Grove, FRGS, Badminton Library, Longmans Green and Co, London, 1895
*Orchesography*, Thoinot Arbeau, Kamin Dance Publishers, New York, 1948
*The Sacred Dance*, W O E Oesterley, Cambridge University Press, 1923
*The Dance,* John Martin, Tudor Publishing Co, New York, 1946
*The Golden Bough*, J G Frazer, Macmillan, London, Abridged edition, 1950
*The Singing of the Travels*, Violet Alford, Max Parrish and Co, 1956
*The Traditional Dance*, V Alford and R Gallop, Methuen, 1935
*European Folk Dance*, Joan Lawson, Pitman, 1953

*The Folklorist*, a magazine about folk dance and song incorporating *The Folk Dancer* and *The Folk Musician and Singer,* published from 1954 to 1964 in Manchester
*Viltis*, a folklore magazine obtainable from Vyts Beliajus, Box 1226, Denver 1, Colorado, USA

*Other sources*
The Vaughan Williams Library, English Folk Dance and Song Society, 2 Regent's Park Rd, London NW1
Society for International Folk Dancing, London. This society arranges courses at which visiting dancers teach the dances of their own countries

Interesting information about folk dances is available from Lt Col Baldrey, 505 Wilbraham Road, Manchester 21

## Festivals in Britain
There is an increasing number of folk dance festivals in Britain to which dancers from other countries are invited to demonstrate their dances, to teach them or to take part in international competition. Those of Llangollen, Billingham, Sidmouth and Tees-side are perhaps the best known. Particulars may be obtained from the English Folk Dance and Song Society.

## Records
The following addresses may prove useful
Interest in foreign records of all kinds
Colletts, 70 New Oxford Street, London wc1
Discurio, 9 Shepherd Street, London w1
Good international folk music recordings are available from
Lyrichord, 141 Perry Street, New York 14 (obtainable from Discurio)
Argo, 115 Fulham Road, London sw3

FOLKCRAFT RECORDS
A catalogue is obtainable from 1159 Broad Street, Newark, New Jersey, USA or from Folkraft Europe, Rue Fr Couteaux, 52B–1090 Brussels, Belgium
Folk Music International, 56 187th Street, Flushing, New York 11365, USA
Topic Records Limited, 27 Nassington Road, London NW3
The Society for International Folk Dancing has made some useful records

## Music
Novello and Co, 27 Soho Square, London w1 issues a catalogue of folk dances and songs.
Those who are interested in folk instruments should visit the Horniman Museum, London Road, Forest Hill, London, SE23. A publication *Musical Instruments* is available.

## Dance descriptions
The descriptions have been made as full as is consistent with clear setting out of the notes. Teaching notes give supplementary information and sometimes also advice on methods of presenting and coaching the dance.

A real attempt is made to indicate the style and quality which alone distinguish the dances of different nations. It cannot be too frequently emphasised that only by observing and dancing with people of the country can the style be fully absorbed, and understood. It is important that the individual dance description is read together with the general information about dances of the country.

## Steps
Advice on the teaching of steps which are common to the dances of many countries has been given in the main text. Before the dances of each country are descibed there is advice on the teaching of steps and variations which occur in a number of dances of that country. For the individual dance there is guidance about steps which are special to that dance or which are danced in an unusual way.

In the individual dance where a step or sequence recurs it is given with its detailed timing once only.

## Abbreviations
These have been kept to a minimum in order that the reader is not constantly interrupted by the need to refer to an appendix. The following simple devices have been adopted,

| | |
|---|---|
| R | *right foot* |
| L | *left foot* |
| O | *outer foot* (In a couple dance the foot further from the partner when the dancers are side by side) |
| I | *inner foot* (In a couple dance the foot nearer to the partner when the dancers are side by side) |
| cw | *clockwise* |
| cc | *counter clockwise* |
| LOD | *line of dance* (Used to indicate the general direction of travel round the room of a couple or similar dance) |

## Relationship of steps to the music
A comma is used to separate the movements of each count, eg 4 running steps forward, R, L, R, L.
The same separation is used for the counts, eg 4 running steps forward, R, L, R, L, COUNTS 1, 2, 3, 4.
When such a sequence is repeated the overall timing is shown, eg repeat the running steps COUNTS 1–4.
Similarly when a step takes more than one count the overall timing is given, eg 1 Israeli walk COUNTS 1–2.
The counts are written over the notes of the music; this gives complete accuracy but teachers are warned that the step will begin to feel right only when it is danced as a whole to the music. Dancers should be led into the steps with the music and the teacher should

resort to analysis only when there are difficulties. Teachers are strongly advised to keep the counts for their own use and to give words of guidance, eg RIGHT-LEFT-RIGHT-HOP in preference to numbers when leading the dancers into the rhythm. It is important to use the voice to suggest the quality of moving as well as to indicate the beat so that the learners will absorb the rhythm and not merely strive to keep in time.

As the counts are marked above the music the same numbers are used for reference in any repeats of the music, even when different steps are used.

## Diagrams

Where diagrams have been used they give an aerial view of the dance. M has been used as the symbol for the man dancer and G for the girl. The symbol has been placed to indicate the direction in which the dancer is facing, eg

|  | Front |  |  | Left |  |
| :---: | :---: | :---: | :---: | :---: | :---: |
| Left | M | Right | Back | ᏻ | Front |
|  | Back |  |  | Right |  |

When the diagram shows the path of the stepping dotted lines have been used with arrows to indicate the direction in which the dancer travels and the new position that he reaches.

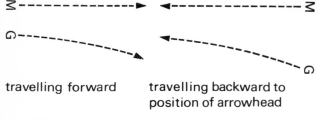

travelling forward     travelling backward to position of arrowhead

When the diagram is used to show the dancers hand holds, uninterrupted lines are used as symbols for the arms with large dots for the hands.

Man with right arm forward and left arm backward to join hands with the girl

Girl with left hand on hip and right arm forward to join hands with the man

## Labanotation—kinetograms of the dances

Where it has been possible to obtain kinetograms, these have been included as an additional aid to the interpretation of the dances. The source and notator of each is indicated.

For two reasons at least the kinetograms may not exactly match the word descriptions since they have not been prepared by the same observer. In many cases the source of the dance was not the same, and typical of folk dance is the local and even personal variation which creeps in. Secondly, the observer is almost certain to bring some personal prejudice to the observing however impartial he tries to be.

Despite these recognised problems it has seemed worthwhile to include the kinetograms, partly to encourage a wider use of notation in the recording of folk dances and partly to offer some interesting material to those who are learning to read notation.

In the future when Labanotation is more generally used, a book such as this may be able to dispense with words and diagrams. On this occasion it has seemed helpful to use all three forms of guidance.

*Books about Labanotation*

*Labanotation: system for recording movement*, Ann Hutchinson, Theatre Arts Books, New York; OUP, London, 1970

*Practical Kinetography Laban*, V Preston-Dunlop, Macdonald & Evans, London, 1969

*An Introduction to Kinetography Laban*, V Preston-Dunlop, Macdonald & Evans, London, 1966

*Handbook of Kinetography Laban: examples*, Albrecht Knust, Das Tanzarchiv, Hamburg, 1958 (out of print)

*Handbook of Kinetography Laban: text*, Albrecht Knust, Das Tanzarchiv, Hamburg, 1958 (out of print)

*Centres for Kinetography*

Beechmont Movement Study Centre, Gracious Lane, Sevenoaks, Kent

Knust's Institute, 43 Essen-Werden, Folk Wang, Hochschule, West Germany

*Dance Notation Bureau*

Miss Ann Hutchinson, c/o Language of Dance Centre, 5 Lincoln's Inn Fields, London WC2, offers a Folk Dance Correspondence Course

# AUSTRIA

*Siebenschritt*

*Studentenpolka*

*Treffner Tanz*

# AUSTRIA

The folk dance movement in Austria is very well organised. The Folk Dance Federation, *Bundesarbeitgemeinschaft Österreichischer Volktanz*, and the provincial associations serve to link together the local groups, and take responsibility for the big regional gatherings of folk dancers. In the early years of this century interest began to centre in the difficult exhibition dances and to provide variety there was a tendency to invent new ones. This led to a loss of interest in the traditional forms. In 1922 Professor Raimund Zoder began to found folk dance groups to counteract the growing inclination to ignore the simple and genuine dances which over the years had given so much pleasure and sense of fellowship to ordinary people.

The Federation, its groups and their leaders, are anxious to preserve the traditional style and pattern of the dances. Herbert Lager, president of the Vienna Association, has written 'Our dance activities are based on the traditional dance; it does not appear to us to be untimely or 'out of a museum'. Therefore we refuse alterations of traditional forms and we believe that impulses expressing our time will bring about a living modification in time'[1].

Many Austrian groups travel abroad regularly to share their dances with the dancers of other nations. The dances are vigorously enjoyed and though they are scrupulously rehearsed they do not lose their naturalness and there is no lack of humour and gusto on practice night.

Clearly a country at the heart of Europe, whose boundaries have often changed, will have dances in common with its neighbours. Austrian dances have marked kinship with those of Bavaria and Switzerland. The 1970 Folk Dance Festival was held in Klagenfurt in honour of Carinthia's fiftieth year as a province. Since it has been Austrian only since 1920 it is natural that some of its dances are shared with neighbouring Slovenia. At the festival was a splendid group of dancers from Süd Tirol, now a part of Italy, but continuing to share the common heritage of dance of the mountain frontier region. On the same occasion a lively group from the province of Burgenland which borders Hungary, and where there are Hungarian and Croatian minorities, played music which showed the folk influence of these peoples.

Nonetheless, Austria is particularly rich in national folk lore and a visitor who is fortunate enough to observe some of the folk customs is better able to understand the dances and the part they play in the country's heritage. An interesting surviving folk tradition, the *Kanzelreiten*, takes place on Whit Monday at Feistritz in the Gailtal. Local young men armed with short spears and riding bareback on farm horses are announced by the sound of a trumpet. In turn they gallop along a narrow pathway left in the ranks of the crowd, and as in jousting, aim a stroke as they pass at a cask fixed to a post at about head height. They then canter round in a large circle to attack again, dropping out of the competition if they fail to score a hit. The winner is he who deals the blow finally causing the cask to disintegrate. The pounding of the hooves as the horses reach top speed, hardly missing those who press forward for a better view, produces an excitement similar to that which must have prevailed at a mediaeval tourney. The spectator feels privileged to share in such an occasion, especially one which may well soon disappear because the number of horses is diminishing as modern farming methods become widespread. The winner of the Kanzelreiten has traditionally the responsibility of organising the *Linden Tanz* which follows. The dancers approach the dancing ground beneath the lime trees in procession as the men sing an old Slovak dance-song, a religious song of benediction. This solemn dance is followed by lively dances which include the *Gailtaler Polka* and the *Treffner Tanz* and later dancing becomes general.

## Style and types of dance

The simple social dances which are known and practised in all parts of Austria are usually couple dances. They are easy to learn and enjoyable to dance. In town or village square or in the ballroom, when large numbers take part, they are also an impressive sight for the spectator, since the tight-packed dancers move with vigour and skill. Rodney Gallop claims that 'the foundation of these, curiously enough, is partly to be found in the old English Country dances which were so fashionable at court in the seventeenth and eighteenth centuries', and he continues, 'Pair dances replaced the old-fashioned country dances from their supremacy in the ballroom, and in the Austrian folk dances of today it is easy to see how these pair dances have been grafted on to the country dance figures as they slowly descended in the social scale until finally they reached the peasants'[2].

In 1956, at a conference in Lienz, it was decided to select twelve traditional dances which should be fostered in every province. Now, when dancers from all-Austria gather together, these dances form the mainstay of the programme. They could well be termed national dances as their practice is so widespread. Two of them are included in this book, one with the attractive variations danced in Süd Tirol. There are many similar social dances, some of them local dances and others more widely known though under differing names and with regional variations.

Apart from these social dances there are many which require much careful practice. They are exhibition dances, included at a social evening while most of the company rests. These are the figure dances with complicated holds and twists, such as the *Steiregger* and the *Steirischer*, fascinating both to watch and to dance. The number and intricacy of the figures in some of these demand close attention and a good memory. They are basically couple dances in which the man leads his partner through a series of involved patterns with a constantly changing relationship of each individual couple; there is interest in the constantly changing relationship of the man and woman as well as in the shapes described by the whole group of dancers. During the course of the dance there may be many changes of partner but the couple is reunited in a final waltz. In all such dances, and particularly in the variety of *Landler* known as the *Schuhplattler*, the men take the major role; the girl dances with downcast eyes while her partner exhibits his rhythmic and acrobatic skill both to her and to the assembled company, from time to time giving further vent to his exuberance in shouts and yodelling. A relatively simple figure dance, the *Treffner Tanz*, is included in this book.

To enjoy the dances of Austria it is necessary to have mastered the Viennese style waltz and be able to dance it smoothly and at speed. A well-balanced position of the couple is essential with feet close and shoulders leaning away. Likewise success in the other characteristic turning step, the two-step, depends on the exact balance of the two dancers. In Austria a free or open waltz or polka brings everyone to the floor and the skill and speed of footwork are remarkable; and so also is the energy and stamina of the older dancers who share the evening enthusiastically with the many young people.

In teaching the Austrian dances good use can be made of the open waltz to give practice in the turning waltz included in a sequence of the couples' own choice, and of the open polka to give practice in the two-step combined with other steps chosen by the individual couples. Control and enjoyment in these spinning movements are revealed when the action causes the girls' full skirts to fly out to the horizontal.

There is no place in this book for a description of the many ritual dances which are still performed, the sword dance of the salt miners of Hallein, the dance of the Perchten, or carnival runners, or the hoop dance of the iron-ore workers of Carinthia. However, the interested visitor should lose no chance of seeing these and similar dances since they offer a real insight into the Austrian folk tradition.

*Costume*

Each of the nine provinces has its own style of costume and many small villages have their own traditional dress. The costume illustrated here is that worn in the Gailtal in Carinthia. It is unusual in showing Slav influence, a reminder that the valley is near the frontier, and in having a short skirt which is said to be worn because the district is so often flooded. The costume has been adopted by the excellent Edelweiss dance group of Klagenfurt whose musician leader is Arnulf Wadl. The costume is appropriate for all the dances which are described in this section of the book.

In every provincial capital there is a folk museum and traditional costumes, *Trachten*, are particularly well displayed in the Tiroler Volkskunstmuseum in Innsbruck and at the Landesmuseum in Klagenfurt. The Director of this Landesmuseum, Dr Koschier is a highly respected folklorist who has written books both on the regional dress of Carinthia and on the folk dances of the province.

*The Trachten* were of homespun materials and sometimes made up by itinerant tailors; likewise shoes were made by the local cobbler for the country people from leather tanned at the farm. Shoes were usually black and both men's and women's decorated with buckles. Leather from chamois or red deer is now used for the knee breeches or short trousers of the men, being tough enough to give long years of wear. Other interesting leather features of the man's costume are the intricately embroidered braces and enormous money-belts. The homespun wool is made into loden and is used for men's jackets and for much of the women's winter *Trachten*. Predominant colours are green and grey which were the traditional hunting colours. The felt hats of both men and women are decorated by feathers of the black cock or hair of the chamois; these decorations were originally hunting trophies.

*Trachten* have survived in the more remote villages and are worn on festive occasions. It is interesting too, to note when window gazing in Vienna or other cities how greatly the *Trachten* continue to influence the shape, colour and detail of the hats, the dresses and the jackets of both men and women. The *Dirndl* in particular is no museum piece; most women have at least one and the summer *Dirndl* worn with a short-sleeved white blouse is to be seen everywhere. Tourists know best the costume of the Tyrol and frequently assume that it is the costume of all Austria just as they tend to think that the Tyrolean *Schuhplattler* is the national dance.

The weight of the gay and colourful costume and the fullness of the girls' skirts have influenced the social dances of Austria since they lend themselves to the smooth waltzing and turning, while the low-heeled shoes are ideal for a stamped accompaniment. The clothes of the men, designed for the rigours of an outdoor life, are turned to account in the *Schuhplattler* which exploits the freedom of the *Lederhosen* in its leaps and kicks and enjoys a lively accompaniment from the hand beating on the leather of shorts and shoes.

## Music

The music of the dances of Austria is for the most part straightforward and cheerful. Since it is regular and must be repeated many times the folk musicians provide simple variations. There are few dance songs, but the *Steirischer* includes some singing as the men dance to the centre with strong clapping and stamping to sing verses often improvised and topical. The women wait demurely, waltzing on the spot or travelling gently round the room, ready to be re-joined by the men for the chorus of the dance. Most Austrian dances are not accompanied by singing; they take at least some of their quality from the four-square, matter of fact, but nevertheless sympathetic, playing of the small folk dance band.

Songs do, however, form an important part of the folk dance evening and are enjoyed by the dancers as they rest, glass in hand, from their exertions. The songs often include yodelling and many are part songs with beautiful harmonies. Great pride is taken in purity of tone and the singers are received with warm and serious appreciation.

The instruments used to accompany dancing vary from province to province. In Carinthia they are most frequently the accordion, the double bass and the clarinet, sometimes with the guitar. The musicians do not merely watch and play for the dancing; they are at one with the dancers and an integral part of the occasion.

Those who were fortunate enough to hear the playing of the Engel Family during their tour in Britain will have been impressed by the number and diversity of Austrian folk instruments, the *Raffele*, a three-stringed instrument from Sud Tirol, the *Hackbrett*, a type of dulcimer, played in all mountain regions and the *Blockflöte*, similar to a recorder and played in Salzburg. The attractive sound of the *Hölzernes C'lachter*, translated wooden laughter, a type of zylophone, is Tyrolean. All are used in the folk music of their own regions. The zither is a more recent instrument, only about a hundred years old; it is not used to play music for folk dance.

The folk music in Austria developed in the family circle during the isolation of long winters in remote, snow-bound villages. Dancing too developed as a family activity and tourists in the Tyrol have for many years been entertained at a *Tyroler Abend* by the versatility of a local family and their friends in dancing and singing in the family hotel or pension.

## References
[1] Herbert Lager, 13th Annual Session of the International Folk Music Council, 1960
[2] Rodney Gallop, 'The Folk Dances of Austria', in the *Dancing Times*, London, May, 1935

## Source of the dances
The dances were recorded in Klagenfurt during visits to several dance groups and during the Bundesvolkstanztreffen, the annual gathering of Austrian folk dancers, at Whitsuntide 1970. The dances were filmed on these occasions and at the traditional Kanzelreiten in the Gailtal.

## Acknowledgment
Most sincere appreciation is recorded of the help given by:

Herr Arnulf Wadl and his sister Mrs Erika Campbell who made the visits possible

Dancers of the Edelweiss Group and the many other participants and organisers of the national folk dance meeting

Miss Verina Verdin who prepared the kinetograms. These are the only kinetograms which are based on dancing by English dancers.

*Bibliography*

IN ENGLISH

*Dances of Austria*, Katharina Breuer, Max Parrish, London, 1948

'The Folk Dances of Austria,' Rodney Gallop, in *Dancing Times*, London, May 1935

'Sword Dances and Secret Societies', R Wolfram, in Journal of EFDSS, Vol. 1 No. 1

*The Traditional Dance*, V Alford and R Gallop, Methuen and Co, London, 1935

*Living Country Customs in Salzburg*, P C Pott-Flatz, Karl Gordon, Salzburg, 1950

*Austria*, Monk Gibbon, B T Batsford Limited, London, 1962

Numbers of *The Folklorist*

*Picture Post* of March 1949 (Schemenlauf, Imst)

IN GERMAN

*Osterreichische Tänze, Volumes 1 and 2*, Herbert Lager, Osterreichischer Bundesverlag, Vienna, 1959 and 1969

*Kärntner Volkstänze, Volumes 1 and 2*, Franz Koschier, Verlag des Landesmuseums für Kärnten, Klagenfurt, 1963

*Lebendige Volkstracht*, Franz Koschier, Verlag des Landesmuseums für Kärnten, Klagenfurt, 1963

*Sources of information*

Austrian Embassy, 18 Belgrave Mews West, London SW1

Austrian National Tourist Office, 16 Conduit Street, London W1

Anglo-Austrian Society, 139 Kensington High Street, London W8

Austrian Institute, 28 Rutland Gate, London SW7

In Austria there are folk museums in most towns. The Tyroler Volkskunstmuseum in Innsbruck and the Landesmuseum in Klagenfurt are of particular merit.

*Opportunities to see dancing*

Many of the folk festivals in Austria take place outside the tourist season but performances of the dances are presented for visitors. The standard and authenticity of such performances vary considerably. There are many folklore groups in Austria concerned to preserve the traditional dances but there are also commercial interests which seek to give the tourist an attractive display of virtuosity and have little regard for tradition. The visitor must be discriminating if he wishes to learn more of the genuine Austrian dance.

Good groups of Austrian dancers visit Britain frequently under the auspices of the Anglo-Austrian Society.

*Records*

*The Twelve National Dances* and many other social dances have been recorded by Schallplattenverlag Walter Kögler, Stuttgart. The *Twelve Dances* are on EP 58 101, 102, 103

*Austrian Folk*, The Engel Family, Fontana, SFL 13213, 6446 001

*Austrian Mosaic*, World Wide, SCX 6266

## SOME AUSTRIAN STEPS AND HOLDS

### Swing step

This is danced in 3/4 time. It consists of a step to the right side on R(1), a swinging across of L with a brushing gesture helped by resilience in the supporting knee (2), and a slight hop on R as the L reaches the crossed position (3). The hop is often reduced to a mere rise on the ball of the supporting foot.

*Teaching*   Good control is needed to keep the movement even. There should be no jerk on the hop which is really very unobtrusive; the lead into the next swing step should be very smooth. The shape of the step is slightly scooping. The raised foot is held easily. In preliminary practice encourage a bold step sideways and perhaps, at first, a scrape of the foot as the leg swings across to ensure that the inside of the foot and leg leads the way. Count,

DOWN-SWING-HOP

and face the class using the opposite foot and emphasising the slight sink on the stepping which helps to fill out the three beats evenly.

### Two-step

As danced in Austria, this step keeps low and is smooth; the steps should melt into each other and into the preliminary steps. Sometimes it is quite difficult to tell whether the Austrians are waltzing or dancing the two-step because in each case the effect is of even, continuous, uninterrupted turning.

*Teaching*   It is essential first to ensure that the couples take a firm well-balanced hold. Before trying the step, test the balance by practising any type of steady turn or spin to show control. It is as well to practise the two-steps in a little sequence like counts 17–32 of *Siebenschritt* so that the dancers do not get giddy and so that they get used to disengaging at the proper time.

### Landler

This is really a swinging walk taken in 3/4 time, filling out the three counts evenly. There is a slight give in the knee as the step is taken and the back foot draws up beside the supporting foot on (3), resting on the ball of the foot ready to take the next step forward. (The *Landler* step in *Treffner Tanz* is a slight variation of this.)

*Teaching*   It is important to give words of advice in a swinging even tone and to fill out the time as,

STEP DRAW UP<br>1    2    3

### Running

The stepping is smooth and natural; there is no sense of bounce and the steps cover the ground.

### Hands

When alone the dancer has hands on the hips or lightly joined in the small of the back with palms facing backward. A man may grip the front edge of his jacket just above waist height.

### Holds

In all normal holds the girl's hand rests on that of the man.

### Waltz grasps

Open hold 1 is used for *Wiener Walzer*, the Viennese waltz. The leading arms are stretched out at shoulder height but they are not stiff. The man's right hand is on the girl's waist and her left hand rests on his right shoulder, or sometimes stays at her side. The girl is held slightly to the man's right side.

Open hold 2 is used in other dances; it is similar, but the man has his right hand on the girl's left shoulder-blade   *Figure 1*

*Figure 1*                                    *Figure 2*

Closed hold is also used when the dancers turn in twos. Both the girl's hands rest on the top of the man's shoulders while he encircles her to put his hands on her shoulder-blades. She is directly in front of him   *Figure 2*

# Siebenschritt

## SEVEN STEPS

This is the best-known of all the folk dances and is danced throughout German-speaking Europe, in Croatia and in parts of Italy. The song is a children's rhyme; the words vary from district to district. Those given by Dr Koschier are as follows:

> Eins, zwei, drei, vier, fünf, sechs, sieb'n,
> Wo fåhrst mit dein Schubkårrn hin?
> Wo denn hin, nåch Berlin,
> Wo die schönen Madln sind.
>
> Bauer, häng dein Schimmel ån,
> Dass er mi nit beissen kånn,
> Beisst er mi, klåg i di,
> Tausend Tåler kostet's di
>
> Brüderlein, komm, tånz mit mir,
> Beide Hände reich ich dir,
> Einmål hin, einmål her,
> Rundherum, dås ist nicht schwer

### District
Danced in all parts of Austria; the variations are from the Süd Tirol.

### Music
2/4 time, regular and even. There are four running steps to the bar. The two tunes written here can be used together.

### Record
Schallplattenverlag Walter Kogler. EP 58 103

### Style
The dance travels smoothly over the ground with little rise and fall. Although it is a couple dance there is also a sense of the big circle and the dancing of the whole group.

### Formation and holds
At the beginning the girl is on her partner's right side and both face cc. Inner hands are grasped at chest height. When the dancers leave each other, the girl has her hands on her hips or in the small of her back, while the man holds the front edge of his jacket. For the two-steps the closed hold is used.

| Steps | COUNTS |
|---|---|
| 7 runs forward beginning O | 1–7 |
| Pause with 1 swinging slightly past the supporting foot | 8 |
| 7 runs backward beginning 1 | 9–15 |
| Pause raising O | 16 |
| *3 runs travelling diagonally forward and away from partner (man toward the centre of the room; girl to the outside) turning their backs slightly to each other | 17–19 |
| Pause raising 1 | 20 |
| 3 runs travelling diagonally forward and inward to meet partner | 21–23 |
| Pause lifting O in preparation for two-step | 24 |
| *Figure 3 a* | |
| 2 two-steps with partner in closed hold, making two complete turns and at the same time travelling LOD | 25–32 |
| Repeat from *. | 33–48 |

### VARIATION A
The same pattern of stepping is used but the ground pattern differs. 7 runs turning away from partner in a little circle to complete two turns and finish facing partner on the pause.
*Figure 3 b*
7 runs turning in the reverse direction to complete two turns and finish facing partner on the pause.
3 runs away from partner to complete one turn and pause facing partner.
3 runs in the reverse direction to complete one turn and pause facing partner.
*Figure 3 c*
The two-steps are danced as in the basic dance

### VARIATION B
The runs are replaced by step sideways and close. Each dancer travels first to the left. The man has his back to the centre of the room; the girl faces towards the centre.
Travelling to own left, step sideways on L and close R to L, 4 times.
*Figure 3 d*

Travelling to own right, 4 step-close beginning R
*Travelling to left, 2 step-close
Travelling to right, 2 step-close
2 two-steps as in the basic dance
Repeat from *.

*Teaching notes*
The runs are quiet and without spring; they cover the ground though long steps should not be used. Note that the steps of the two-step are slower, ie the complete two-step takes a whole bar of four counts. It is important that the dancers are ready for the two-step so that they may step boldly into the turn. In variation B as she returns from the side steps, the girl must close up the L to take the weight and so free the R

for the two-step; when the man closes he should retain the weight on R so that he may step round his partner into the two-step. A simplified version of the two-step section is sometimes used in which running steps are used for the turn and partners stand with right shoulders together, hands are joined and right arms are straight and held across the front of the partner, while the left elbows are bent. Hands are at shoulder height.

In variation A the dancers trace small circles with the stepping and do not merely turn about on the spot. As the partners turn from each other the outer shoulder pulls back to lead into the turn. To ensure control it is essential that the dancers really see each other as they come to the pause and are face to face.

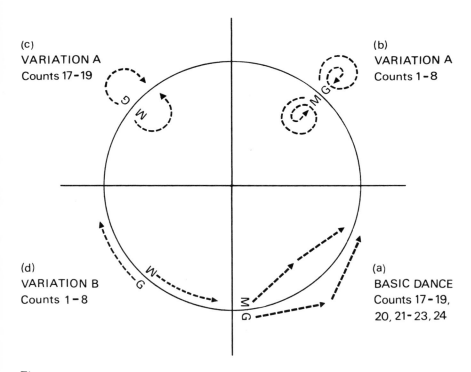

(c)
VARIATION A
Counts 17-19

(b)
VARIATION A
Counts 1-8

(d)
VARIATION B
Counts 1-8

(a)
BASIC DANCE
Counts 17-19,
20, 21-23, 24

*Figure 3*

43

## Siebenschritt

Notation from *Österreichischer Tänze, erster Teil*

# Siebenschritt

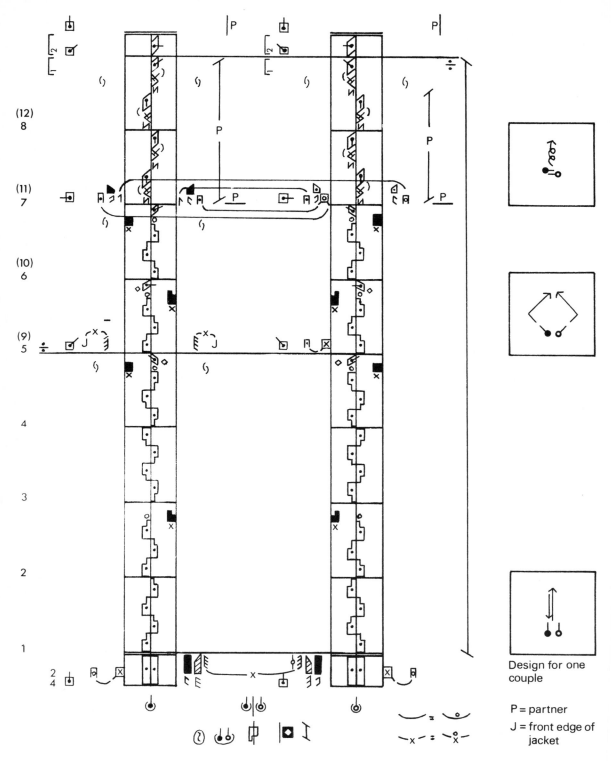

Design for one couple

P = partner
J = front edge of jacket

# Variation A

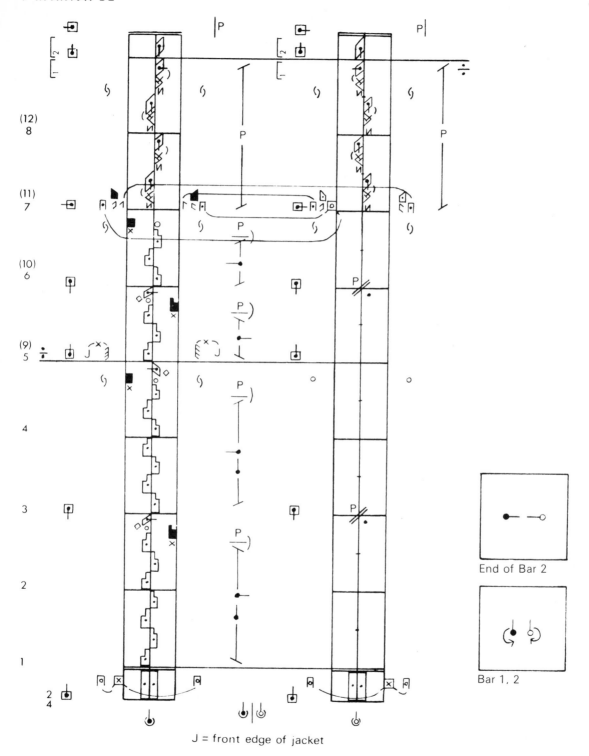

End of Bar 2

Bar 1, 2

J = front edge of jacket

# Siebenschritt Variation B

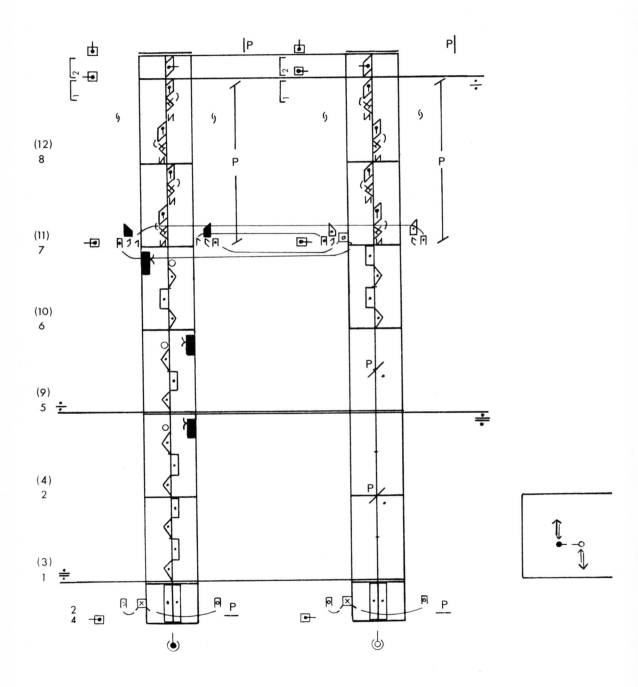

# Studentenpolka

This dance seems originally to have been danced by one girl between two men whereas now the central dancer is a man. The first record of the dance is in 1763.

*District*
Danced throughout Austria.

*Music*
This is unusual in that section A is in 3/4 time, while section B is in 2/4. The two sections are therefore in sharp contrast. The two tunes 1 and 2 may be used alternately to give variety as the dance is repeated many times.

*Record*
*Schallplattenverlag Walter Kögler* EP 58 103

*Style*
Part A is swinging with resilience in the step. Part B flows smoothly over the ground, keeping level.

## PART A
*Formation and holds*
The man is in the centre holding the girls by the hand. All face and travel cc. The stretched arms swing forward and back; the girl's free hand is on her hip. The man first faces the inner girl as he swings his left arm back; he then faces the outer girl as he swings his right arm back.

| *Steps* | COUNTS |
|---|---|
| The man takes a swing step L turning to face the inner girl who takes a swing step R, (their raised legs swinging towards each other), while the outer girl steps R and slightly turns her back to the man. | A 1–3 |
| Man takes a swing step R and turns to face the outer girl who steps on L. The inner girl steps on L and slightly turns her back to the man | 4–6 |

Dance the sequence 7 more times progressing LOD.

*Figure 4*

## PART B
On the up beat * the hands are freed, ready for the change.

*Formations, holds and steps*
The step is a quiet gliding run which indoors may be replaced by walking step. The man links elbows with each girl as he dances with her.

| | |
|---|---|
| Man dances with outer girl linking right elbows, while inner girl turns cw on the spot. All use 4 runs. | B 1–4 |
| Man dances with inner girl linking left elbows, while outer girl turns cc on the spot. All use 4 runs. | 5–8 |

*Figure 5*
Dance the sequence 3 more times.

*Figure 5*

# Studentenpolka

*Teaching notes*

In part A the man begins by swinging his left arm back and his right arm forward. He then changes both his arms as he turns to the other girl; this produces a continuous pendulum swinging. The girls may lean slightly back during the swing step. All is easy and unforced.

In Part B the man travels in a continuous figure eight and the lone girl, having turned about, is ready to offer her elbow as he comes to her.

Attention must be given to the change from part A to part B and back as the dancers will find it difficult at first to adjust to the constant changes of time.

## Studentenpolka

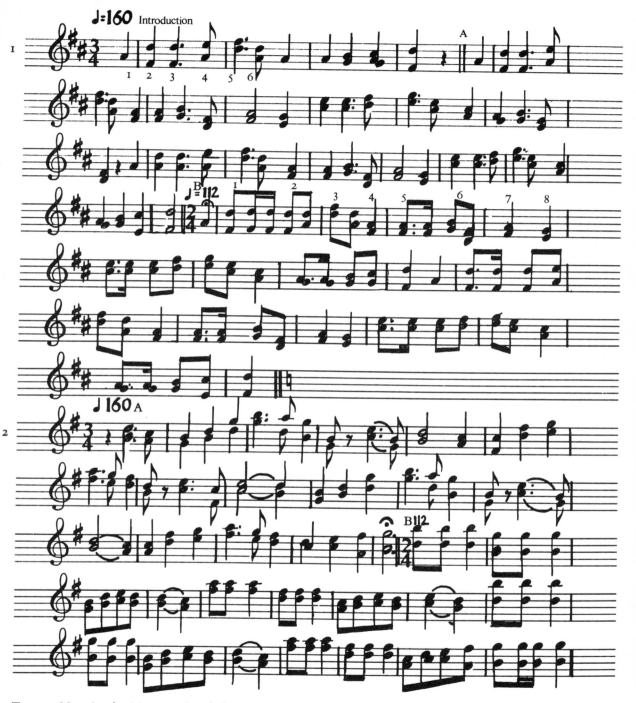

Tune 1. Notation by Margaret Smith from Record EP 58 103 *Schallplattenverlag Walter Kögler*
Tune 2. *Österreichische Tänze, erster Teil*

# Studentenpolka

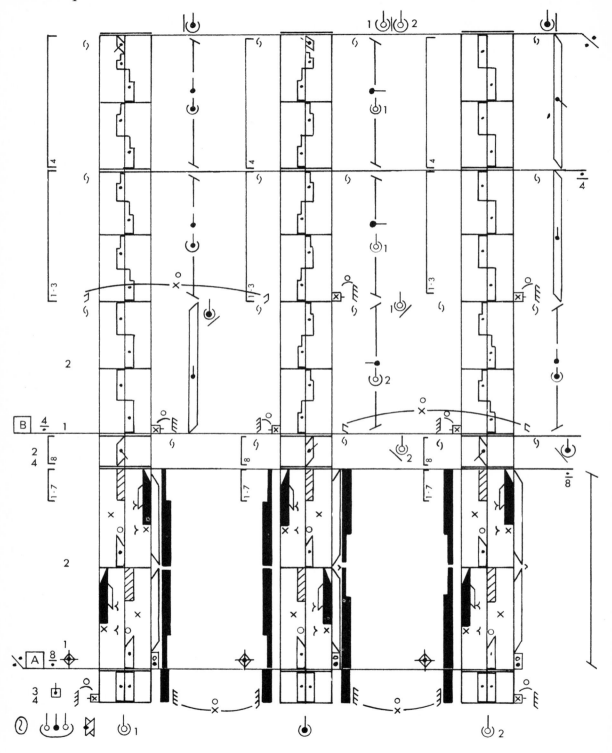

# Treffner Tanz

*District*
Carinthia (Kärnten). The dance originated in the small market town of Treffner.

*Music*
In a very regular, swinging 3/4 time. For the complete dance the sections of the music should be played in the following order,

   A B   C D E  A B  A B  A B  C D E  A B  A

Since each *landler* step takes 3 counts, ie one bar, the timing of this dance is set out in bars.

*Style*
A circle dance for 6 couples in which the interest centres in the ground patterns, since the step, a variant of the *landler* step, does not change.

*Formations and holds*
Most figures are danced first cc and then cw. Skilful dancers will not need to break their hold until the end of part c.

*Step*
*Landler* step with the back foot picked up gently but clearly on the 3rd beat of the bar. The heel leads in the forward step; the foot is put down with care and the

effect is slightly stealthy. The step may be danced forward, backward or sideways according to need in the dance. In the sideways stepping, the foot crosses in front. The character of the step is maintained throughout.

*Figure 6*

## PART A
*Big circle*
The girl is on the right side of her partner. Dancers face and move to the right. Hands are joined and the left rests on the dancer's own hip, while the right reaches forward to the hip of the dancer ahead.
8 *landler* steps beginning R          BARS A I-VIII

*Figure 7*

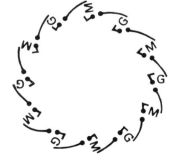

*Figure 8*
*Big circle*

Dancers face left and move cw.
Now the right hand is on the dancer's own hip while the left reaches forward to the hip of the dancer ahead.

8 *landler* steps          BARS A IX-XVI

## PART B
*Girls' arms over*
Dancers face and move cc. The man keeps his left hand at his hip but, on the first step, with his right hand he lifts the girl's left hand over her head to rest on her right shoulder.
8 *landler* steps.
On the 8th the man lifts the girl's hand back over her head.          BARS B I-VIII

*Figure 9*

*Figure 10*
*Girls arms over*

Dancers face left and dance cw. The man keeps his right hand at his hip but, on the first step, with his left hand he lifts the girl's right hand over her head to rest on her left shoulder.
8 *landler* steps.

On the 8th the man lifts the girl's
hand back over her head.          BARS B IX-XVI

## PART C1
*Men's star*

The man lifts his right hand high and turns under it
leading with the right shoulder. He turns to the left
until he faces the outside of the circle and lowers his
arms so that they are straight and crossed in front of
him (the right over the left). The men are now
shoulder to shoulder and with their backs to the
centre; each looks forward between two girls.
4 *landler* steps                 BARS C I-IV

*Figure 11*

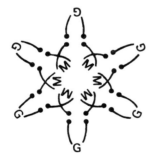

*Figure 12*
*Men's star*

The formation moves cc.
4 *landler* steps sideways         BARS C V-VIII
The formation moves cw.
4 *landler* steps sideways         BARS C IX-XII
Man lifts the right hand high; he turns to
the right under the arm and goes out to
form the big circle once again.
4 *landler* steps                 BARS C XIII-XVI

## PART C2
*Girls' star*

The same figure exactly is danced by
the girls                    BARS C XVII-XXXII

## PART D
*Girls' wheel*

Girls turn to face cc, freeing the left hand from the
partner and resting it instead on the wrist of the girl
ahead. The men join in a small circle round the girls
who rest their right hands on the joined hands of the
men. All arms are stretched. The formation travels cc.
8 *landler* steps                 BARS D I-VIII

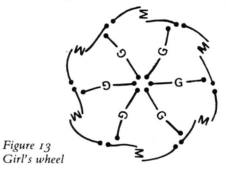

*Figure 13*
*Girl's wheel*

The girls turn about swinging the right to the centre
to take the wrist of the one ahead and resting the left
hand on the men's joined hands. The formation
travels cw.
8 *landler* steps                 BARS D IX-XVI

*Figure 14*

## PART E
### Double circle
The girls change from the wheel to form an inner circle which travels cw; their hands are held as in *Big circle*. The men's outer circle moves cc. The men stretch both their arms out but the girls hold the right hand at the hip.

8 *landler* steps                    BARS E I–VIII

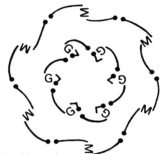

*Figure 15 Double circle*

Everyone turns about and repeats the figure in the other direction. The girls now have the left hand at the hip.

8 *landler* steps                    BARS E IX–XVI

## PART F
### The chain
The girls remain in their circle, face the centre and stand with hands high to make gateways. The man leader frees his right hand and goes through the gate made at his partner's right side; he draws the line of men after him, winding in and out of the gateways in a cc direction.

16 *landler* steps                    BARS A I–XVI

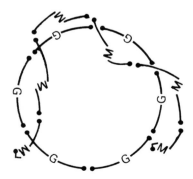

*Figure 16 The chain (at* BAR XIV*)*

The men continue to weave in and out but now dancing singly with hands on hips

16 *landler* steps                    BARS B I–XVI

## PART G1
### Men in and clap
The girls continue to make the gateways. Each man with his hands on his hips dances through the gateway on his partner's right side and claps his hands on the first beat of the 4th bar (marked ★ in the score).

4 *landler* steps                    BARS A I–IV

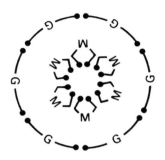

*Figure 17 In and clap*

Each man turns and dances out through the next gateway to his right.

4 *landler* steps                    BARS V–VIII

Continuing to travel in and out in a cc direction, the men repeat the sequence twice.

8 *landler* steps                    BARS A IX–XVI

8 *landler* steps                    BARS B I–VIII

Then the men travel to the centre through the gateway at partner's right hand side and clap.

4 *landler* steps                    BARS B IX–XII

They remain in the centre and raise their hands to form arches.

4 *landler* steps                    BARS B XIII–XVI

## PART G2
### Girls in and clap
The same figure exactly is danced by     BARS A I–XVI
the girls and at the end
the big circle is reformed.              BARS B I–XVI

*Figure 18* BAR V–VIII

## PART A2
*Big circle*
As danced in A1                    BARS C1–XVI

## PART H
*Lead across*
The circle remains unbroken as one couple leads across and through an arch made by the dancers opposite. The leading couple travel back to their own place by making an arch of their leading arms and carrying it over the heads of all the other dancers who have followed them across the circle.

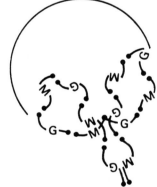

*Figure 19*
*Lead across*

16 *landler* steps                  BARS C XVII–XXXII

## PART A3
*Big circle*
As danced in A1                    BARS D I–XVI

## PART E2
*Double circle*
As danced in E1                    BARS E I–XVI

## PART I
*The basket*
The men lift their hands over the heads of the girls in the inner circle. The girls' joined hands will then be across the men's waists. The men's arms will be in front of the women at shoulder level.

8 *landler* steps sideways to the right     BARS A I–VIII
8 *landler* steps sideways to the left      BARS A IX–XVI

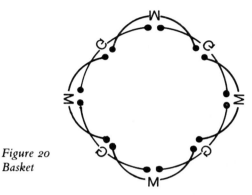

*Figure 20*
*Basket*

## PART J
*The crown*
The men lift their hands back over the girls' heads and bend down to make a seat for the girls on their joined hands. The girls rest their arms on the men's shoulders.
The men lift the girls                BARS B I–IV

The circle travels cc.
4 *landler* steps sideways            BARS B V–VIII

The circle travels cw.
8 *landler* steps and the girl leaps
lightly down on the 8th               BARS B IX–XVI

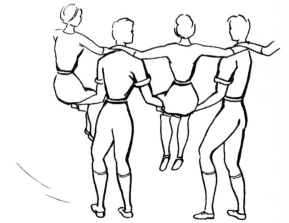

*Figure 21*

57

## FINAL

The couples dance away with turning waltz steps in the open hold.

*Teaching notes*

When the dance is really well performed the onlooker is aware of the movements of the group but hardly notices individual dancers. To achieve this standard the dancers must know the figures very well.

Avoid making a feat of memory of this dance or the dancers will lose the sense of steady continuity which makes the figures attractive. Each figure can be a little dance in itself.

Avoid also too mathematical a division into bars; the dancers should be guided into the changes by a feeling for the phrasing of the music. The teacher will need to warn the class well ahead of the change that is coming, timing her instructions so that they finish just as the new figure is due to start. The dancers should swing naturally into the claps and the changes of direction as the result of easy dancing and not through tense counting.

## Treffner Tanz

Notation by Margaret Smith from a tape recording made in Klagenfurt

# Treffner Tanz

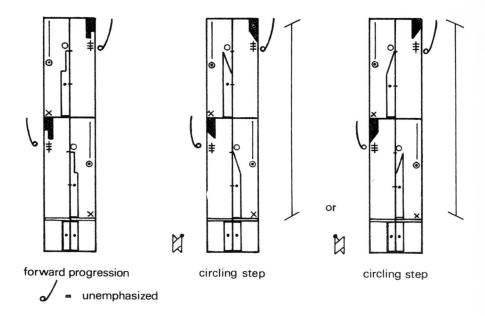

forward progression       circling step     or     circling step

= unemphasized

This dance consists of a simple step repeatedly used in a variety of changes in the group pattern. As these patterns are already given in the diagrams accompanying the word descriptions, it is of no advantage to repeat them in Labanotation. Therefore, only the basic step is notated here.

# FRANCE – BRITTANY

*Jabadao*

*Laridé de la côte*

*Polka piquée*

# FRANCE—BRITTANY

Since the Middle Ages Brittany has had a high reputation for her songs and dances. The dance for which Brittany was then famous was the *Trihory*, described by Thoinot Arbeau in *Orchesographie* in 1588. It is described too, by Léandre Vaillat in his *History of the Dance* as being a gay dance in duple time, light, coquettish and playful through the way in which the left foot, always the left, advanced gliding and reaching along the floor like the paw of a young cat. This description would serve well still for the leading of the left foot in the *jabadao*. The *trihory* was the *Breton branle* and the present day *passe-pied* is derived from it.

It is said that the people of Brittany dislike sudden change and have therefore absorbed new patterns and steps in dance very gradually, welding them to the existing dance. Breton dance has not been destroyed during the centuries because the Breton people have a strong sense of tradition and so have been able to safeguard the essence of their dances. Pierre Hélias says that they took what pleased them from any source, giving little thought to its origin, but incapable of slavish imitation, their importations failed to alter the underlying character of the Breton dance and instead were bent to its rhythm, pattern and nature[1].

For the same reason all the dances of a particular district preserve a family likeness even when they bring together elements of widely differing quality; since all is filtered through the original inspiration it achieves unity with the existing dance style.

Undoubtedly there has been constant inter-action between the popular *haut-danse* with its leaps and turns and the court dance, more ceremonial, more measured. At the court the tunes were made over and the choreography revised to become the *basse-danse*; then as the fashion faded the dance returned to the peasants, but with a new lustre and polish, some of which was retained as the dance became again more lively in the manner of the *haut-danse*. It seems to have been the women who preserved the quality of *basse-danse* which many of the Breton dances still show, while the men more naturally returned to the *haut-danse*.

A fresh interest in the dances of Brittany was aroused in 1896 at Saint-Brieuc during a revival of Celtic folklore and bardism. From this revival have grown the numerous *Cercles Celtiques* of today which are chiefly responsible for keeping alive the practice of the dances and for the preservation of their traditional forms. Dances are still being discovered and the young people in the groups are encouraged not only to dance and to sing but also to study the origins of the dances and to seek out older people in the country districts who remember songs and dances from their youth.

The first of the *Fêtes des reines de Cornouaille* was held in 1923. The success of this festival led to renewed interest in the dances both in the countryside and among the large group of Bretons living and working in Paris, where in 1930 they founded the *Korollerien Breiz-Izel* (Dancers of Basse-Bretagne). Members of this group shared knowledge of the dances of their home districts with each other and also returned to Brittany to study more; as a result Madame Galbrun in 1936 wrote down descriptions of the most characteristic dances. In 1963 Jean-Michel Guilcher's very detailed study *La Tradition populaire de danse en Basse-Bretagne* was published and interest in the wealth of dances and their variations continues. There is a Breton federation for folklore which is one of eleven affiliated to the *Confédération Nationale des Groupes Folkloriques Francais*.

*Style and types of dance*
M Cadenet, Bard of Honour, wrote in 1943, 'The abundance of different types of dances in Brittany and their undoubted character of antiquity leads us to believe that Brittany is the only Celtic country where traditional Celtic dances have persisted in their nearly original form, the main reason for this being very probably that Brittany has not been invaded as many times as the other Celtic countries by foreign people with their own folklore and dances'[2].

As a general rule, the dance in those parts of the country which were rich and more open to the influence of the town is *basse-danse*, gracious and contained, because the growth of a middle class brought the desire to adopt the manners of the aristocracy. In the poorer districts where there was a wholly peasant society the *haut-danse* lingered. Dancing changes between the mountain region and the coast; as it moves it loses its violence and its leaping to become more leisurely in pace. The dance is more deeply felt in the mountains: it has more elegance in the richer lands near the coast. The nature of the soil has also affected the dance; just as the man of the mountains does not walk in the manner of the man of the plain, so his dancing also differs.

As ancient dances all have had some special significance, but in recent years, as the country way of life has altered, they have changed or lost this inner meaning. Many of pagan origin now have a Christian significance. The *Jabadao*, for long disapproved by the Church, so that dancers risked excommunication in taking part in this popular dance, has ceased in this century to be regarded as improper. Though the *Jabadao* has been thought by some to be of very ancient origin, J-M Guilcher has found no evidence of this, though he gives instances of strong prejudice against the dance as late as 1905[3].

The gavotte maintained its popularity in Brittany after it went out of fashion elsewhere and gavottes in Brittany today are as varied as they are numerous. Some are danced in circle or chain formation while others are for two or four dancers; the steps also differ but all include the *pas dreo*. Madame Galbrun suggests that the circling movement of this step is derived from the *rond de jambe* which introduced the reverence, or bow, in the court gavotte of Louis XIII.

Some of the many other characteristic forms of dance are the *bal*, the *dérobée*, the *jabadao,* the *ridée* or *laridé*, the *passe-pied, rond* and *gigouillette*. Some dances are known as *gavotte d'honneur* or *danses des rubans*; these are competition dances for which the prize may be a ribbon, a kerchief, or for a man, tobacco. For a woman ability in the dance adds to her attractiveness and is regarded as proof of intelligence and good health. In Brittany champion dancers, like champion wrestlers, are regarded as local heroes.

In learning the dances it is important to retain the grace, elegance and measure of reserve which are characteristic. There is a gaiety and aplomb about these dances and despite the traditional dress the Breton dancers give no sense of the museum. The girls dance with eyes cast down and the men lead them confidently through the figures by the firmness of the hand grasp. The man is somewhat of a dandy. He grips the edge of his jacket with the thumb of his free hand. All movements are exact and sometimes rapid; they are marked at times by a sharp beat of the foot. The dancers are lively and animated.

*Costume*

The larger folk dance festivals in Brittany are preceded by a procession, or *défilé* in which many hundreds of dancers take part. In Quimper the procession takes the greater part of a morning to promenade through the streets. Some sixty groups of dancers led by their *sonneurs* and accompanied by nearly thirty *bagads* (bands of pipers) form the parade. All are in traditional costume whose beauty is amazing, with rich colour, lovely lace and splendid embroidery.

The women's coiffes first attract the onlooker. They vary in size and shape but all are elaborate. Lightly constructed of starched lace over tulle, they may be very tall as in Pont l'Abbé, winged as in Pont Aven, or small and neat as in the costume illustrated here which is that of Haut-Bretagne, worn in Nantes. The head-dresses frequently are decorated with ribbon and have streamers of lace or ribbon hanging down behind. The men's hats are black with broad brims and flat or rounded crowns. They may be decorated with velvet, used either as trimming or in streamers.

The men's trousers are wide and made often of pin-striped material. Very full breeches of stiff-gathered, heavy white material are worn in some districts in place of trousers. Jackets and waistcoats are usually black but in some districts they are dark red or of natural shade. They vary greatly in length and in cut but most seem to be decorated with rows of buttons, both down the front and on the sleeves; decorative sections or edgings of the jacket may be made of velvet. Sometimes a broad black or coloured waist band is worn.

Women's skirts are full and of quite heavy material, reaching to the calf. In some costumes embroidered velvet is used for the skirts. With all the dresses there is an apron; usually it is large and of the same length as the skirt but small embroidered aprons form part of some of the costumes. Some aprons have a bib which covers the front of the bodice. Many of the costumes are worn with a large shawl and in some districts the shawl has a long fringe. Many of the bodices are decorated with lace which may form large epaulettes or be worn as a fichu or a large kerchief. With some of the costumes lace gloves are worn.

Everyday shoes, usually black, are used for dancing though until recently wooden sabots were worn and are still in use for some forms of farmwork. In earlier times these sabot were finely decorated with carved and painted flowers and leaves and were often given as wedding presents.

The range of colour and style is immense. All costumes are worn with a sense of pride but with absolute naturalness so that the wearer gives no impression of dressing up. The *défilé* is an impressive sight and there is no doubt that the attractive costumes have helped to reawaken interest in the dances.

In presenting dances it is essential to choose a costume appropriate to the region where the dance is usually performed. Beautiful books of costume, good postcards are available, and frequently in advertising local attractions, the *Syndicat d'Initiative* distributes leaflets featuring the regional costume. Every year a poster is issued which features the previous year's *Reine de Cornouaille* and shows the coiffe in great detail.

There are a few places in West Finisterre and in Morbihan where traditional costume is still worn everyday. In Loire Atlantique, Côtes du Nord and in Ille et Vilaine older women continue to wear the coiffe although they no longer wear traditional dress. The visitor to Brittany is not likely to be disappointed in his search to see dancers in their local dress.

## Music

The dances are accompanied either by singing or by two *sonneurs* playing the *biniou* and the *bombarde*. The *biniou* is similar to the Scottish bagpipes but its sound is lighter and so easier for dancing. The *biniou* which is used by dance groups in Nantes is called a *veuze*. It is the traditional *biniou* of the region and has a single drone instead of the more usual three. The *bombarde*, a type of rustic oboe, plays the melody. The airs are simple and well-marked.

Pierre Hélias says that the music of the *bombarde* and the *biniou* with their curious minor mode communicate a feeling of effervescence to the hearer which compels him to dance. It is not therefore surprising that *sonneurs* have been accused of witchcraft. Noël de Fail in the sixteenth century recorded that they were termed 'sellers of wind by the pound' and that, though popular with the people, they were disapproved by officialdom, despite the religious origin of the dances which they accompanied[4].

Mrs Grove describes the accompaniment to the dances in 1895, 'Dancing begins to the sound of the traditional biniou, while near the chapel or fountain sits the orchestra on a moss-grown dolmen. The peasants cannot however always have an orchestra. Occasionally they wish to dance a rond or passe-pied and no sonneur is present, in lieu of whom they take an ivy leaf, roll it round and whistle into it, holding it between their teeth. Some sing while others dance, or they sing and dance together'[5]. Whether this use of a leaf continues in Brittany or not, the author was told by a folklorist visiting Austria of one such player in Yugoslavia still.

Now players of the *bombarde* and *biniou* are hard to come by as many prefer to play as part of a *bagad*, the Breton band which is composed of *binious*, *bombardes* and drums. For those who enjoy the music of these bands there is an international festival at Brest each year with thousands of participants.

At the *Festou Noz*, or night dances, held most often in mountainous regions, the dance songs engender the community spirit. The song is begun by one of the dancers, to match exactly the rhythm of the dance; this singer, the *kaner*, improvises a refrain in what is known as *tralalalaleno* which has the quality of the mouth-music of the Scottish Highlands; the song is taken up by a second voice, the *diskaner*, and at times the whole company of dancers may join in. The singers improvise verses until their invention gives out and then the dancers continue to the sound of their own feet until the singers take up the song. To be successful the singing must be in complete accord with the mood of the dancers. Each area has its own particular cadences and the rhythms are subtle. This music provides a lively forceful accompaniment until the singer-dancer gives up for lack of breath.

The Breton groups always practise to the sound of the *biniou* or to their own singing. A piano accompaniment would be unsuitable but the tunes are simple enough for the teacher to ask the dancers to accompany themselves. Indeed in mastering the trick of the *laridé* the dancers will find it especially helpful to sing as they dance.

*References*
[1] Pierre Hélias, *Danses de Bretagne,* Editions d'art, Chateaulin, 1965, page 6
[2] M J de Cadenet, 'Traditional Dances of Brittany', *Dancing Times*, London, 1945
[3] Jean-Michel Guilcher, *La Tradition Populaire de danse en Basse-Bretagne*, Mouton and Co, Paris, 1963, page 469–470
[4] Pierre Hélias, *Danses de Bretagne*, page 18 and page 14
[5] Lilly Grove, *Dancing*, page 266

## Source of the dances

The dances were first filmed at the *Fêtes de Cornouaille*, Quimper in 1969, and also at the *Fêtes des Bruyères* in Fougeres. In 1970 M and Mme Hautebert of Nantes were kind enough to arrange for long discussion and the opportunity to dance with the group, *Tréteau et Terroir*. A further occasion for more detailed filming was the visit of Mme Hautebert and the group, *Javelle du Pays d'Ancenis* to Llangollen.

## Acknowledgment

Most sincere appreciation is recorded of the help given by:

M Gérard Hautebert, Président de la Fédération Bretagne des Groupes Folkloriques Français

Mme Jacqueline Hautebert, La Sécretaire, Conseil Scientifique des Groupes Folkloriques Français

Dancers of Tréteau et Terroir (Groupe Haut-Breton de Nantes), Oliviers de Clisson, and La Javelle du pays d'Ancenis

Madame Jacqueline Challet-Haas who supplied the kinetograms

## Bibliography

IN ENGLISH

*Dances of France*, Part 1, C Marcel-Dubois and M M Andral, Mas Parrish, London, 1950

*Dancing*, Lilly Grove, FRCS, Badminton Library, Longmans Green & Co, London, 1895

*Orchesography*, Thoinot Arbeau, Kamin Dance Publishers, New York, 1948

'Traditional Dances of Brittany', M J de Cadenet, *Dancing Times 1945*, reprint of article dated 1943

*Folk Tales of France*, Editor Geneviève Wassignon, Translater Jacqueline Hyland, Routledge and Kegan Paul, London and University of Chicago Press, 1968

*The Land of Pardons*, Anatole le Braz, Methuen, London, 1906

IN FRENCH

*La Danse Bretonne*, Erwanz Galburn, Carhaix, 1936

*La Tradition Populaire de danse en Basse-Bretagne*, Jean-Michel Guilcher, Mouton and Co, Paris, 1963

*Danses de Bretagne*, Pierre Hélias, Editions d'Art, Chateaulin, 1965

*Coiffes de Bretagne*, Pierre Hélias, Editions d'Art, Chateaulin, 1967

*Pardons de Bretagne*, Florian le Roy, Jos le Doaré, Chateaulin, 1960

*Costumes de Bretagne*, Pierre Hélias, Editions d'Art, Chateaulin, 1969

*Dansez la France, Tome 1*, M Decitre, Editions Dumas, Saint Etienne, 1963

*Danses de Provinces de France, Tome 3*, Bouch, Gest and Simbron, Editions Jacques Vautrain, Paris, 1946

*Histoires et Légendes de la Bretagne mystérieuse*, Claude Tchou, Editeur, Paris, 1968

## Sources of information

French Embassy, 22 Wilton Crescent, London, SW1

The Breton Centre, Sloane Street, London, SW1

French Government Tourist Office, Piccadilly, London, W1

In France there is a Syndicat d'Initiative in every place of any size.

## Opportunities to see dancing

The ideal time to see Breton dancing is at a village festival. The most typical Breton gathering is the Pardon which is a religious celebration in honour of the patron saint of the local church. M Cadenet says 'Together with religious celebrations like masses, benedictions and processions, a great deal of dancing takes place'. Information about these can be obtained in the locality if the inquirer is sufficiently persistent. Fêtes at larger centres are advertised at the Syndicat d'Initiative though it is difficult to find any but local information. A leaflet *Fêtes Folkloriques en Bretagne* is edited by *La Fédération des comités des fêtes folkloriques Bretonnes*. Visitors should also try to attend a Festou Noz at which the dancing is traditionally accompanied by song.

## Records

Obtainable from Wolf-Lenoan, 4 Rue Astor, Quimper, Brittany

*Mouez Breiz*, Disque No 3325

*Mouez Breiz*, Disque No 3132 for Tralalalaleno

*Dix Dances Bretonnes*, Dek Koroll Breiz, LDM 10 001, Disques Vogue

*En Passant par la Bretagne*, Vega Folklore, Stereo 19 159

*Chants et danses*, Treteau et Terroir

*En passant par la Bretagne*, Folklore de France, Dux 40476

*Mouez Breiz*, Disque No 30–347, Recorded at the Pardon in Plévin, a village in Haut-Bretagne

## SOME BRETON STEPS AND HOLDS
### Gavotte step
This is made up of three steps followed by a hop. It is counted evenly

RIGHT—LEFT—RIGHT—HOP

The steps flow into each other. On the hop the lifted foot is at the side of the supporting foot whatever the direction of travel. There is no extension of the foot.

*Teaching* The step should be practised in every direction and turning so that the dancers acquire the control to change direction at will. The foot action should be kept well under the body with no large leg gesture which might upset the balance.

### Pas dreo
This gives character to the sequence of steps known as the *grand pas de gavotte*. On the *pas dreo* the front foot draws an arc in the air by moving forward, outward and round to finish behind the supporting foot, ready to cut under; at the same time the dancer rises slightly on the ball of the supporting foot (count 1).

*Figure 22*

The circling foot then replaces the supporting foot to take the weight (count 2). The circling action is carefully controlled and smooth. It is accompanied by an opening out of the shoulder of the same side so that the dancer's whole side appears to take part in the circling, though he remains facing forward. There is some sense of lingering over the *pas dreo*. The dancers must have the skill to control the body weight over the foot in rising and in lowering as balance is required to master this step and swing into the remainder of the *grand pas de gavotte*.

*Teaching* The dancers should draw the shape of the circle with the right foot and slip it under the left, several times. Then they should try to put the *pas dreo* into the pattern of the *grand pas de gavotte*. It is best for the teacher to dance in front with her back to the group, looking over her shoulder to see that the dancers are making progress. The class may practise with the left foot circling though this does not happen in the dances; the teacher must be able to use the left foot so that she can face the class and dance with them. If the dancers find the controlled rise and fall on the left leg very difficult, the teacher will have to devise some practices to help.

### Polka
This is a travelling step though each of the component steps covers only a short distance. The feet do not close up and so the step has the nature of marking time. There is no spring and the minimum of rise and fall.

### Hands
In *laridés* the dancers link with a little finger hold, the girl's finger placed on the man's. In other grasps she places the palm of her hand on his. Men hold the lapel of the jacket with the free hand. Girls' arms hang naturally at their sides and they grasp the skirt between finger and thumb.

### Arm swinging
Arm swinging is an interesting feature of many Breton dances. The swing is never free-flowing but is firm and accurate with exact timing. Typical of the group of dances called *laridés* is a stressed interruption in the sequence of swings. The rhythmic pattern of the arm swing is often different from that of the stepping.

# Jabadao

The *jabadao* was for long regarded as a work of the devil. The word is derived from the Breton word for *sarabande*, the dance of the devil.

## District
It is danced in most parts of Brittany. The figures vary in different areas. The version described here is danced in Finisterre.

## Music
In $\frac{2}{4}$ time. The *biniou* tunes for the dance are divided into 2 sections. The *grand pas de gavotte* is danced to the A section, which is of 8 bars duration; the figures are danced to the B section, which consists of 16 bars.

## Record
*Disques Vogue* LDM 10 001. *Ducretet Dux* 40476. Note that these recordings do not provide for the same number of figures as in this version.

## Style
It is a round dance which 'opens and closes like the petals of a flower'. The dance is gracious but without affectation. The *grand pas de gavotte* is smooth and flowing; it is danced as a chorus between each figure. The figures are danced with more vigour and with some real elevation. It is best if 4 couples take part as each girl then returns to her own partner.

## PART A
### LE GRAND PAS DE GAVOTTE
*Formation*
Each girl is at the right side of her partner in a close circle. Hands are held at shoulder height and elbows are bent. The girl's hand rests on that of the man. The circle travels cw.

| *Steps* | COUNTS |
|---|---|
| Gliding step sideways on L | A 1 |
| Step R across in front of L | 2 |
| Step again L | 3 |
| Rising slightly on L carry R in a little circle to finish behind L ready to cut under. *pas dreo* | 4 |
| Bending the left knee step on R in place of L | 5 |
| Glide sideways L | 6 |
| Step R across in front of L | 7 |
| Rise on R with L lifted slightly | 8 |

Dance this *grand pas de gavotte* once more.

## PART B
*Formation and steps*
This figure is danced into and out from the centre.

| | |
|---|---|
| 1 gavotte step forward, beginning L | B 1–4 |
| 1 gavotte step backward R | 5–8 |

Repeat the sequence 3 more times.

## PART A
Danced as before.

## PART C
*Formation and steps*
With one gavotte step the man dances round to face his partner and to take her right hand in his. She takes her gavotte step sideways to her left.     B 1–4

*Figure 23*

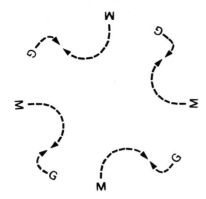

*Figure 24*

*Figures 25*

*Figure 26*

Dance the sequence 3 times more.

PART A
Danced as before.

PART E
*Formation and steps*
Each couple dances to the centre with inner hands joined and lifted forward and up to lead. The whole of the back of the arm is in contact with the partner's arm. The dancers look over the inner shoulder at each other.
1 gavotte step forward on 0.

With 1 gavotte step he dances backward to his place bringing the girl across in front of him to his left side; she makes a complete turn to her left as she crosses over.
Dance the whole sequence 3 times more. Each time the man brings the girl who is on his right side across to his left.

PART A
Danced as before.

PART D
*Formation and steps*
The steps and the ground pattern are exactly as in part C but the man fetches the girl with both hands. Again she completes the turn to her left as she crosses over.

5–8

B 1–8

*Figure 27*

Each couple dances away from the centre opening the arms to a rounded position backwards. 1 gavotte step backwards on 1.

5–8

*Figure 28*

Dance the sequence 3 times more.

PART A
Danced as before.

PART F
*Formation and steps*
Repeat part B but with increased speed and vigour. The style becomes staccato and the arms swing forward and backward with firmness. 4 swings to each gavotte step (forward, backward, forward,

backward). All finish with a last high swing to stand with the joined hands held high.

*Teaching notes*
Although there is no spring in part A, the step is so danced that looking at the movement of the whole circle it is hard to tell whether the dancers are leaving the ground since the whole group 'breathes'. Well danced, the *grand pas de gavotte* has a rippling quality. It helps to count,

SIDE–CROSS–SIDE–CIRCLE–UNDER–SIDE–
CROSS–RISE

singing the words to the tune.

In parts B and F the man marks the first count of the gavotte step with a sharp heel beat.

In parts C and D the man greets each girl with an inclination of head and body as he brings her across. In part C he strengthens the hand grasp by holding the forearms in close contact. In part D the man gathers the girl to him as he takes both her hands; the hands too are drawn close together and the elbows are well down. The man takes care to guide the girl to her new place and to help her to complete her turn.

All figures are bold and open. The dancers cover the ground but they always keep the feet well beneath them.

Dancers need practice in guiding and controlling a partner in all the holds of the dance before they try the figures of the dance. It is helpful to use the holds for the preliminary practices of the gavotte step.

This is quite a difficult dance and the secret of good dancing lies in making the constant changes of direction look leisurely even though the music is fast.

Notation by Margaret Smith from a tape recording made at Llangollen

# Jabadao. Part A

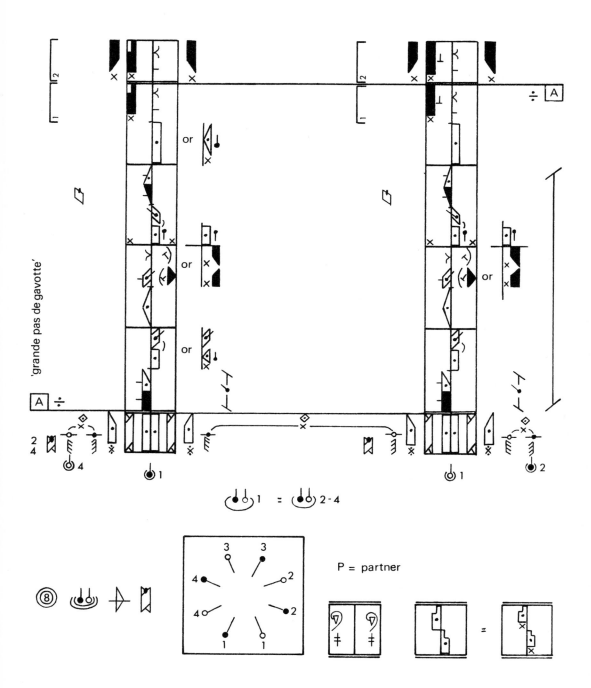

'grande pas de gavotte'

P = partner

# Jabadao. Part B

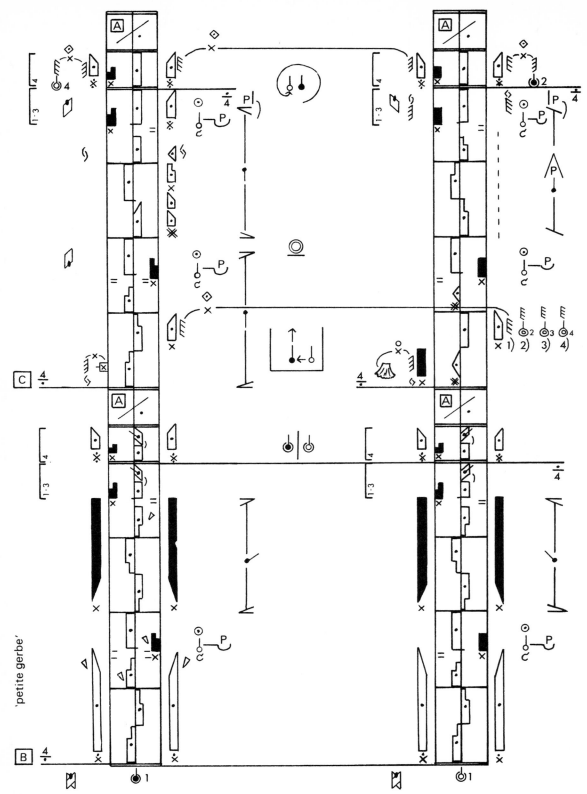

'petite gerbe'

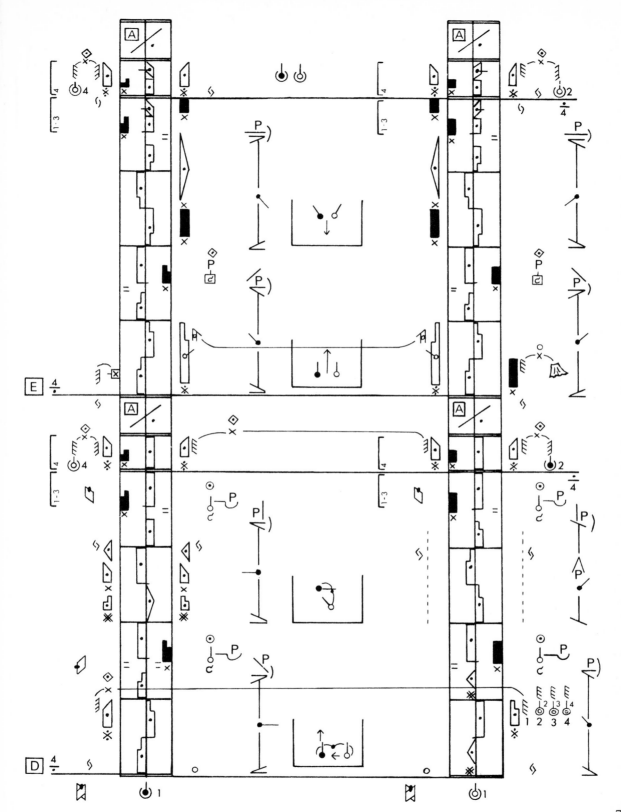

# Jabadao

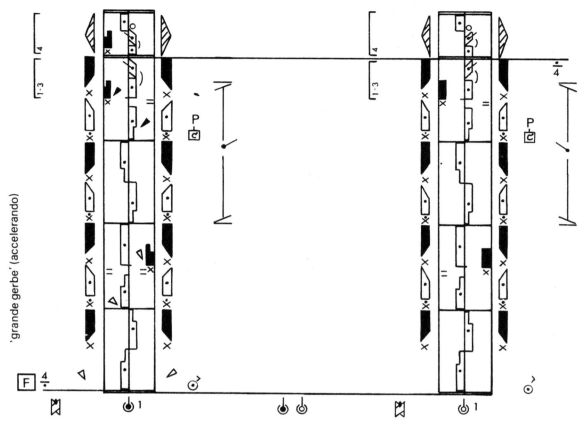

'grande gerbe' (accelerando)

# Laridé de la côte

This is one of many *laridés*, dances derived from the gavotte. Their characteristic is a swinging arm movement which goes with lively stepping. The circle travels always to the left. The name may come from the likeness of the action to a wave poised and ready to crash down on itself.

## District
Morbihan, where it is the typical dance of the region.

## Music
4/4 time with four steps to the bar.

## Record
*Mouez Breiz* 3325

## Style
Lively and crisp with purposeful arm swinging and clear definition of each step.

## Formation
An immense closed chain. The dancers, alternate men and girls, link little fingers and face the centre. The girl places her little finger on that of the man. Elbows are bent and the dancers are shoulder to shoulder. The circle travels cw.

| Steps | COUNTS |
|---|---|
| Step to side on L. | I |
| Step on R beside L. | 2 |
| Step to side on L. | 3 |
| Close R to L with weight evenly divided. | 4 |
| Pause. | 5 |
| Rise on the balls of both feet and quickly lower heels again (a little bouncing action). | 6 |
| Step to the right on R. | 7 |
| Hop on R swinging L across. | 8 |

## Arm action
From a slightly forward position the arms swing as follows:

| | |
|---|---|
| a little back | I |
| forward | 2 |
| back | 3 |
| up to shoulders | 4 |

*Figure 29*

| | |
|---|---|
| Pause | 5 |

With an emphasis bring the hands over forward and then:

| | |
|---|---|
| downward | 6 |
| back | 7 |
| forward | 8 |

## Teaching notes
This is a dance which the teacher must lead by dancing herself. She must therefore have mastered it so completely that she can dance in either direction and maintain the rhythm while talking to encourage the dancers. With a big group she should dance in front with her back to the class. The stepping alone should be practised until the class has picked up the pattern. The teacher must be able to analyse in order to help individuals but only much guided practice will bring results. Helpful words spoken in the rhythm are needed, such as

SIDE—CLOSE—SIDE—TOGETHER—HOLD—BOUNCE—
RIGHT—HOP

When the dancers feel confident and have sensed the rather jaunty character of the movement they will be ready to learn the arm swing, accompanying it with a little bounce in the ankles in order to keep the whole body 'alive'. It is important to begin from a position in which the arms are lifted slightly forward. Again guide with words as

BACK—FORWARD—BACK—UP—HOLD—OVER—
BACK—FORWARD

When the dancers can keep the rhythm going successfully with the arms they will enjoy working at swing and stepping together. Full pleasure in this dance comes only when the dancers are so certain, that the movement carries them along. It is wise to delay the use of the close chain until the dancers are quite confident, though if one novice joins a skilled group of dancers, the close formation helps to transmit the rhythm and the correct sequence.

Notation by Margaret Smith from a tape recording made in Nantes

*Laridé*

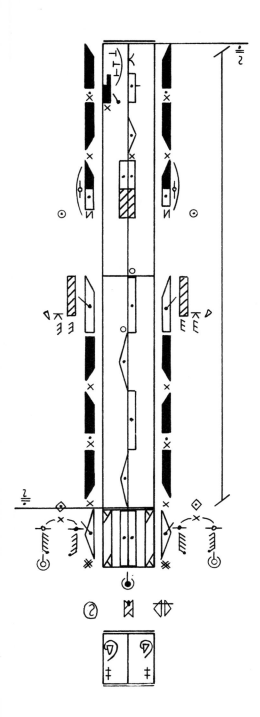

# Polka piquée

The dance commonly known in England as *polka piquée* is in fact the Breton *Gigouillette* and is danced in most parts of Brittany. *Polka piquée* is, in various forms, known throughout France and especially in the provinces of Poitou and Le Centre.

*District*
*Polka piquée* is danced in Haut-Bretagne but not in Morbihan, nor in Finisterre. The two versions described below are from the Loire-Atlantique; they may be danced immediately following each other.

*Record*
*En passant par la Bretagne*, Vega Folklore, stero 19 159.

*Music*
Light, gay and well-marked in 2/4 time.

*Style*
A couple dance travelling in a circle clockwise, the LOD for all Breton dances.

VERSION A
## CHATEAUBRIANT
*Formation and holds*
Partners stand back to back; the man faces the outer side of the room, the woman the centre. Their near hands are joined and held high over the leading shoulder.

| *Steps* | COUNTS |
|---|---|
| PART A | |
| Place 1, ie the leading foot along LOD on the heel. | A 1 |
| Touch the ground in the same place with the ball of 1, turning the knee in. | 2 |
| *Figure 30* | |

*Figure 30*

*Figure 31*

1 polka step beginning I and turning to
face partner while the raised hands
swing down and back to shoulder height.       3–4
Repeat the sequence beginning with o
and turning back to the starting position
with hands held high on the polka.            5–8
Dance the whole sequence once more.

## PART B
1 polka step sideways on I remaining
back to back.                              B  1–2
1 polka step sideways on o turning to
face partner as the step begins.              3–4
Repeat dancing alternately back to back then facing,
with arm swinging as in part A for 6 more polka steps.
As the A section of the music begins again the inner
foot is brought through for the heel–toe action.

## CLISSON
*Formation and holds*
The girl is in front of her partner and both face LOD.
The man takes both the girl's hands from behind and
holds them slightly above shoulder height and a
little out to the side; her palms rest easily on his.
*Figure 31*
As they dance the man brings the girl across in front
of him, leading her towards and away from the
centre and turning her in to look at him.

*Steps*                                    COUNTS
Using R make the heel–toe action as in
Chateaubriant, placing the foot
diagonally forward and towards the
centre.                                    C  1–2
1 polka step R travelling diagonally
forward and to the centre. The man
brings the girl across to be a little to his
right and swings her so that she looks at
him over her left shoulder.                   3–4
Repeat the sequence beginning L and
travelling diagonally forward and
outward on the polka. The man brings
his partner across to his left.               5–8
Dance the whole sequence once more.

## PART B
Using polka steps the couple travels
diagonally forward to alternate sides
beginning R and travelling right. The
girl moves across her partner as in part A.  D  1–16

*Teaching notes*
Little ground is covered in this dance. Its character
comes from the constant change of relationship
between girl and man. The heel–toe action is small
and takes place quite near the supporting foot. The
action is marked by a slight bounce in the supporting
knee.

In the high arm position in *chateaubriant* the backs
of forearm and upper arm are in contact.

The arms in *clisson* are tilted as the girl crosses to
make it easier to see her partner.

## Polka Piquée

Notation by Margaret Smith from a tape recording made in Nantes

*Polka Piquée*

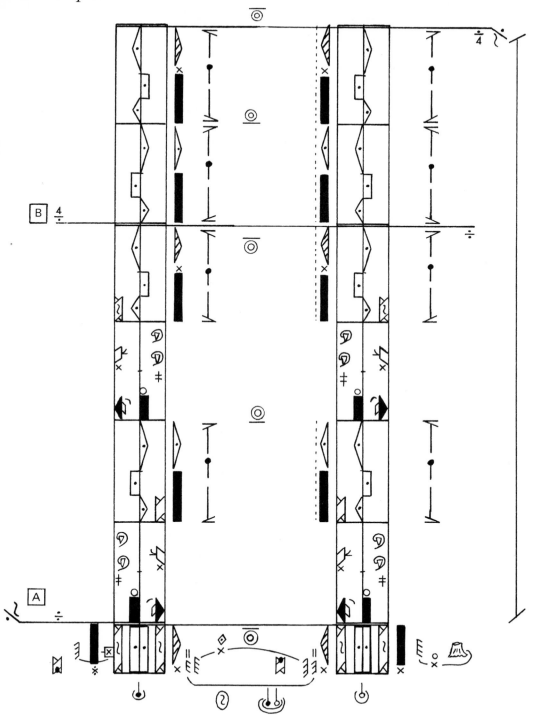

# Polka Piquée

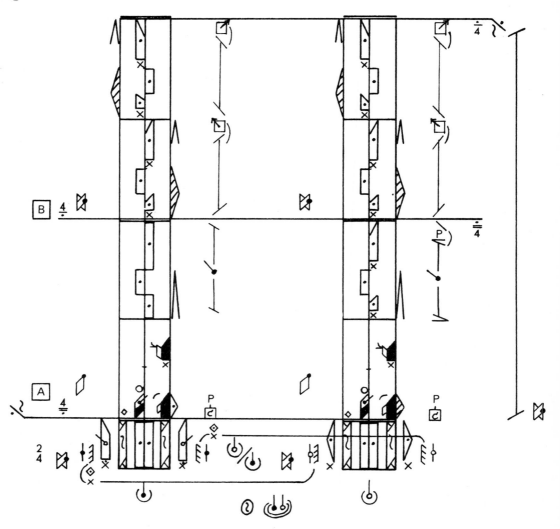

# GREECE

*Baidoúska*

*Two Tratas of Megara*

*Tsakonikos*

# Kalamatiaos

Notation by Jacqueline Challet-Haas

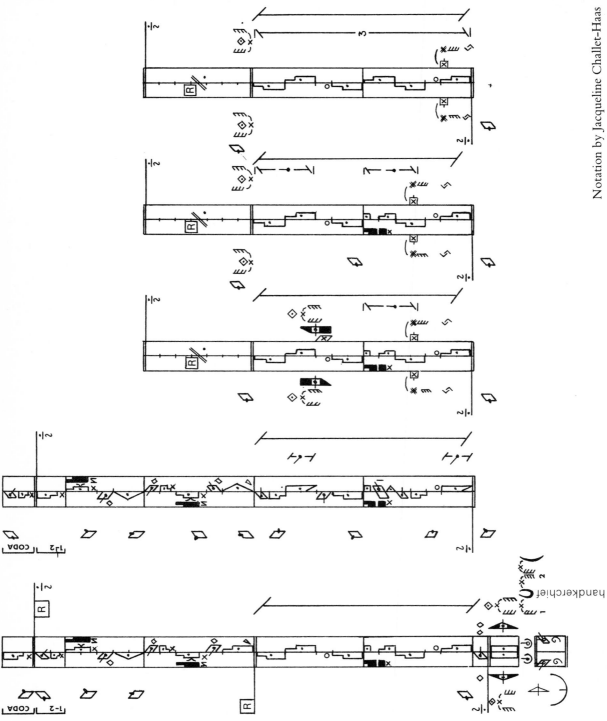

handkerchief

84

# GREECE

There still remains in Greece much evidence of the ancient origins of dance. A walk round the pottery rooms of the National Archaeological Museum in Athens reveals many vases decorated with the figures of dancers. One vase, given as a prize in the eighth century BC, is inscribed 'He who dances better than the others will receive this'. In Lillian Lawler's book, *The Dance in Ancient Greece* there are many excellent illustrations of dancing as depicted in Greek art and a most thorough discussion of the dances of the ancient Greeks.

In the introduction to *Fifty Greek Dances* (the authoritative work on the folk dances), C Sakellariou writes, 'Youths and maidens at the religious rites at Knossos, welcomed the coming of spring with dance. Draped maidens danced at the feast of Demeter and at the feast of Argive Hera. Maidens too danced for Artemis at Karyai and at the Panathenaic Festival for Athena. At Delos, paid dancers were sent from distant states to honour the god. In all ancient cities, at all religious feasts, "the dance was set" as Pindar says, for Dionysos, and the dithyramb was the most honoured among the dances. In those days Dance was religion, prayer, worship and faith.'[1]

In the classical age religious, dramatic, athletic and popular dances were performed in temple, theatre and stadium and of these ancient dances some thirty can be traced to the present day. A glance at the calendar of events in 1970 issued by the National Tourist Organisation, gives evidence of a similar diversity of occasions when the people dance in every region of Greece, at festivals of the church and of the rural year.

## Style and types of dance

Since the dances are immensely varied in character, it is possible here only to generalise about the style of Greek dance. For those who wish to teach these dances there are, however, a number of points to bear in mind.

First, the Greeks move and dance with natural, good poise, erect but unforced. They are proud of their traditions, proud of being Greek. The dance style reflects the nation's love of freedom and admiration of the independent spirit. Without this splendid bearing the dances lose their true character. The poise is also derived from the wearing of magnificent costume and the desire to show it to advantage. A slight rotary movement serves to move the woman's dress. For the man, the full heavy skirt enhances the leaps and turning movements while the wide sleeves emphasise the toss of the arm and swirl of the handkerchief.

The handkerchief is used a great deal in Greek dances, held not only in the free hand of the leader where it seems often like a flag directing the chain, but also between the leader and the other dancers, giving him greater freedom of action as he improvises in leaps and twists. Sometimes members of the chain also hold the corners of handkerchiefs instead of joining hands. In villages, by tradition, those who are not related do not join hands. The handkerchiefs may be held by some of the dancers or by all of them.

Foot placings have a natural elegance and care. There is no marked extension but the ball of the foot often leads. There is ankle play and the movement is felt through the foot to produce the flowing quality of many of the dances. Steps are small and for the girl, simple but subtle. She is modest and dances with downcast eyes. The man takes the lead in the dance as he still does in village life; he can improvise and exhibit his skill. If the leader's handkerchief is tossed to him, each man in turn may become the leader and so have the chance to demonstrate his virtuosity.

The last word on style must go to Dora Stratou, who has done so much to arouse interest in the Greek dance tradition, and whose dancers have performed each summer since 1959, first in the Piraeus and now in Athens. She writes, 'One must also appreciate that in all these—music and singing and dancing—there are little peculiarities—vocal tricks here, a special twist of the body there—all depending on the particular area or even the particular village, that are impossible to reproduce. One must simply be born and bred with it.'[2]

In the Greek dances, more than any others in the book, teachers and dancers too, should look for the opportunity to learn from and to dance with those who have been 'born and bred with it'.

Most dances are in closed or open circle formation or in a winding chain. There are some couple dances known as *antikristos*, but these are popular mainly in Cyprus. The chain dance is thought to have spread from Greece, where it originated as the choros circling, first the threshing floor at country festivals, and later the Greek theatre as the classical chorus. The Greek word for dance *choros* becomes in Bulgaria *horo*, in Roumania *hora* and in this form has become the name of one of the most popular groups of dances in the new state of Israel.

The best known dance in Greece, and one which is danced throughout the country, though with local variations in step and tempo, is the *kalamatianos*. No programme of Greek dances would be complete without it. Since descriptions of this dance are available in Britain already, it has not been included in this collection, but its kinetogram has been printed on page 84.

*Kalamatianos* is a *syrtos*, though it is more lively than many in this group of dances, which are called dragging dances to indicate that they travel close to the ground and rarely include springing. In fact the steps do not drag or scrape but they are restrained and without leaps.

The *sousta*, or *pediktos*, form the other group of dances and they include hopping or leaping. Such dances are common in the islands. They are lively in contrast to the calmer *syrtos* and some are derived from war dances.

There are dances which combine some of the elements of each type of dance style.

The individual dances are often given the name of the village of origin or of the district where they are danced. There are, for example, many dances called *kritikos*, dance of Crete. Other dances carry the names of people, often of saints, or they are named for trades or guilds.

The dances in this book were selected to show variety in the use of rhythms and unusual ways of dancing across the musical phrase. They are short and easily learned and give the dancers the opportunity quickly to experience one of the real joys of folk dance which comes when the dancer ceases to concentrate and is carried along by the dance itself.

## Costume

Traditional dress is worn on feast days and at weddings but only a few of the older people still use it as every day wear, though it was generally worn, except in cities, until the beginning of the twentieth century.

There is great variety and each village has its characteristic dress. For this reason it is important that dancers realise that each of the dances described here, in Greece would be danced in a different costume. The traditional dress of Attica which is illustrated in this book does however show the man's costume typical of mainland Greece where in most districts the *fustanella*, or full-pleated skirt, is worn together with a sleeveless jacket of red, blue or purple, richly embroidered with gold or silver and worn over a white shirt with very full sleeves. The uniform of the well known *Evzones*, or Royal Guards, is an example of this costume; their *fustanellas* are white but in some parts of Greece blue skirts are worn. In the islands baggy trousers, known as *vraka*, are worn in which the gathered material is tucked into the waistband. These are black or dark blue.

The woman's dress is usually of thick material; as she is also weighed down by quantities of heavy jewelry there is little jumping in women's dancing. The costumes of the islanders are of lighter material and consequently the dances seem to be higher and gayer. There are many elaborate head-dresses but the headscarf is widely worn and tied in a variety of ways according to the district.

It is possible in Athens to buy articles of genuine costume, both in shops and markets and from the occasional street vendor. The dressed dolls which are widely on sale give some impression of shape and style but, except for the most expensive, are of poor materials which lack weight. Many postcards with photographs of costume are available in Greece and also most attractive hand-painted cards, but these vary in their degree of accuracy.

In the Benaki Museum, a whole floor is given to costumes of Greece. Many are presented on models and it is possible to study all the details of their construction and decoration. The Museum of Decorative Arts, Monastiraki, also has an extensive collection of costumes, very well exhibited; the jewelry is especially interesting. An exceptionally good collection of northern Greek costume is to be found in the Folklore Museum in Thessaloniki, and the Museum of the University of Thessaloniki exhibits splendid embroidery and jewelry, including very elaborate belt buckles.

Madame Kapsambalis kindly sent the following translation of the particulars of the woman's dress of Megara exhibited in the Benaki Museum, 'This costume is the wedding dress worn by the women of Megara on all festive occasions. The skirt, dark green for the young women and dark blue for the elderly, has a large number of perpendicular pleats. At the bottom, to enhance the decorative effect, there are ten to fifteen wide horizontal pleats which add to the richness of the effect. The short coat (*zibouni*) which in older days was of green woollen cloth, later on came to be made of red velvet. This garment was sewn and embroidered locally by craftswomen specially skilled in this type of work. A characteristic feature of this costume is the small fez decorated with silver Turkish coins, which formed part of the wearer's dowry. There are sometimes as much as two hundred coins, sewn on in successive rows which run all round the fez. On her forehead the Megara bride wears a row of golden florins, the gift of the bridegroom. On the crown of the head, attached to the fez is a circular silver-gilt brooch adorned with coloured stones, called the *tasi*. The fez is held in position by a red velvet band embroidered in gold, called kapoutsali.'[1]

## Music

The Greek music is intriguing to the western ear with its unusual rhythms, which are related to the poetic metres of ancient Greek writers. Dora Stratou tells us, 'Greek folk music has fused the remnants of ancient Greek scales and of Byzantine ecclesiastical music, gradually assuming its own unique identity. Greek folk music is basically monophonic and in free scales . . . The characteristic Greek rhythms are 5/4, or 5/8, 7/8, 9/8, the very same metres we find in the tragedies of Aeschylos and other ancient writers. The musical metre was based on the poetic metre, determined by the long and short syllables.

'These rhythms also have different variations in their composition. Sometimes the 7/8 metres have first the 3/8 followed by the remaining . . . 4/8. The next time the reverse may be true. The same holds for the 9/8 metres. The mood and rhythm of the dances change radically according to these changes in metre.'[3]

While the rhythms rightly fascinate the teacher, it is probably wise to avoid any reference to their strange quality at first. In fact, inexperienced dancers are often unaware of the complication and get carried along by the movement if they are skilfully taught. They will be conscious of the attractiveness of something unusual in the music which they may well later enjoy analysing. In the Ionian Islands, which include Corfu, the influence of western music has been more strongly felt and the tunes and rhythms consequently sound more conventional.

The dancing often follows the underlying rhythm rather than the melody, and then the change from one part of the dance to the next is determined by the leader who cries, 'Opa'. The parts of the dance do not then correspond to particular sections of the music. The music and the dance seem to stop unexpectedly, with no sense of warning and of drawing to a close, but with a down stroke of the bow.

A curious point about the music at a feast is that the musicians may be requested to play a particular dance tune by any one of those present, who then owns the dance; only he and his friends may join in and even if he does not choose to get up, no one else may dance.

The small orchestra which accompanies dancers on the mainland is the *zygia*. The instruments are usually clarinet, violin, lute, *santouri* and drum or tambourine. The *bouzouki* and guitar are used in the city night clubs to accompany popular dances including the *zeibekiko* and the *hassapiko*.

The large drum is called a *daouli* and is used mainly out-of-doors when it is often played with the *pipiza*, a shrill shepherd's pipe. The *santouri* is a stringed dulcimer which is struck with two cotton covered beaters. The strings are divided by bridges into different lengths. The small pottery drum is the *doubli*. Except in Crete the lyre has been superseded by the violin. The Cretan lyre is very popular; it is held vertically on the musician's knee as he stands with his foot resting on a stool. The clarinet has taken the place of the shepherd's pipe.

Appropriate accompaniment for the dances is of the greatest possible importance if the class is to dance with appreciation of the Greek style. Gramophone records may be used both to accompany the dances and to help the dancers to understand the nature of the Greek dance music. Stringed or wind instruments will catch some of the magic but the dancers' own singing will probably provide the best accompaniment. It is impossible to dance in Greek style to the music of the piano.

*References*
[1] C Sakellariou, *Fifty Greek Dances*, Athens
[2] Dora Stratou, Introduction to Programme of Greek Dances, Theatre of Philopappos
[3] Dora Stratou, *The Greek Dances*, Athens, 1966, page 32
[4] V Alford and R Gallop, *The Traditional Dance*, Methuen and Co, 1935, page 1

## Source of the dances

A number of the dances including the Easter *trata* and *baidouska* were studied at the Lyceum Club of Greek Women in Athens during a series of rehearsals and at two performances, in traditional costume, given in the Piraeus. The others were danced and their detail filmed, also in Athens, during three meetings with Miss Maria Kinigou.

## Acknowledgment

Most sincere appreciation is recorded of the help given by

Madama Kapsambalis and the men and women dancers of the Lyceum Club, Athens

Miss Maria Kinigou, Athens

Miss Phrosso Pfister, London College of Dance and Drama

Mr Rickey Holden, Folk Dance Consultant, Texas, USA, who supplied the kinetograms

## Bibliography

*Fifty Greek Dances*, C Sakellariou, Athens

*The Greek Dances, our Living Link with Antiquity*, Dora Stratou, Athens, 1966

*Folk Dances of the Greeks*, T and E Petrides, Exposition Press, New York, 1961

*Dances of Greece*, D Crossfield, Max Parrish, London, 1948

*Greek Folk Dances*, R Holden and M Vouras, Folkraft Press, New Jersey, 1965

*Myth and Ritual in Dance, Game and Rhyme*, L Spence, Watts and Co, London, 1947

*Greek Calendar Customs*, G A Megas, Athens, 1963

*Folk Art in Greek Macedonia*, A Kyriakidou-Nestoros,. Balkan Studies, 1963

*The Dance in Ancient Greece*, Lillian B Lawler, A and C Black, London, 1964

*Vasilika, A Village in Modern Greece*, Ernestine Friedl, Holt Rinehart and Winston, New York, 1962

## Sources of information

The Royal Greek Embassy, Press and Information Office, 49 Upper Brook Street, London, W1

National Tourist Organisation of Greece, 195–197 Regent Street, London, W1

National Tourist Organisation of Greece, odos Karageorgi Servias 6, Athens

In other parts of Greece, local tourist committees and the tourist police.

## Opportunities to see dancing

The national Tourist Organisation of Greece issues a calendar of events which includes information about dates of dance demonstrations and of festivals at which folk dance in costume will take place. Village festivals usually take place on the day of the patron saint. Many of these are not included in the official calendar and the traveller is likely to have the thrill of coming upon them unexpectedly. The Tourist Organisation states 'Today in every village and town, on the mainland, in the islands and even Asia Minor ancient Greek territorial feasts, anniversaries, family rejoicings are all accompanied by dancing and song'.

In Athens the interested dancer must not miss the performances throughout the summer by the Dora Stratou Dancers, in the Theatre of Philopappos, nor lose any chance to see the less frequent demonstrations by the Lyceum Club.

## Records

In choosing records in Greece where there are very many on sale, it is important to select genuine folk music and not the popular songs by the stars of the moment, though these are often interesting too. Any of the larger records shops will give helpful advice.

*Greek Folk Songs and Dances*, Dora Stratou, RCA Victor LPMG 9

*Folk Songs and Dances around Greece*, Dora Stratou, Olympic CPTG 50000

*Songs and Dances of the Greek Mainland*, Lyra 3217

There are a number of other good records by this company.

*Greek Folk Music*, Lyrichord, LLST 7188, LL 188

From Folkraft LP3, LP6, LP8   Both 6 and 8 were recorded in Athens.

# Baidouska
## PIGEON-TOED

### District
Danced in Romilia, Macedonia but the dance is of Bulgarian origin.

### Music
The dance takes 4 bars of 6/8 time. This phrase is split in an interesting way into three sections of:
1 one and a half bars
2 two half bars
3 one and a half bars.
The sections match the three changes of direction in the step sequence.

### Style
Lively but firm. Steps are quite small and the weight is contained well over the feet. The back is held firmly and arms are straight and steady but not stiff.

### Formation and holds
The line faces front and travels to the left then, after dancing on the spot, the dancers turn to face the right and move back toward the starting place, so little progress is made. At the beginning the hands are joined and held to a low diagonal forward. The body leans forward with the back held straight and firm.

*Figure 32*

As the dancers turn to face the right there is a sense of lift through the body and the hands are held down. See figure 34

| Steps | COUNTS |
|---|---|
| Facing forward, travelling to the left | |
| Step on R across in front of L. | 1–2 |

*Figure 33*

| | |
|---|---|
| Step to L to the side. | 3 |
| Repeat these two steps. | 4–6 |
| Step on R across in front of L. | 7–8 |
| Hop on R while the left knee lifts and swings to the front with a twist. | 9 |

*Figure 34*

89

Step on L in front of R.                                     10–11
Hop on L while the right knee lifts and
swings to the front with a twist.                                12
Step on R in front of L.                                     13–14
Hop on R while the left knee lifts and
the dancers turn to face the right.                              15
Step and hop 3 times beginning on L
and travelling towards the start.   16–18, 19–21, 22–24

*Figure 35*

The final hop forms the lead in to the repeat of the
dance.

*Teaching notes*

The teacher should master the unusual use of the
musical phrase which gives this dance its character so
that she can lead the dancers into the rhythm, eg,

> CROSS-AND, CROSS-AND, CROSS
> (long-short, long-short, long)

> SKIP-OVER, SKIP-OVER
> (short-long, short-long)

> SKIP-BACK, A-LONG, THE-LINE
> (short-long, short-long, short-long)

> AND
> (short)

The dancers may later be interested to discover the
way in which the music is used but at first they should
simply be led into the dance.

Repeat the dance many times so that the rhythm
grows on the dancers. The first part of the sequence
keeps level and rather low and contrasts with the
upwardness of the skipping to the right. There is no
exaggeration of the twist, but a natural step across
into the turned skips. The turned skips may be
practised alone and counted HOP, CROSS. The end
dancers swing a handkerchief with a circular motion.

As danced by the Lyceum Club for purposes of
demonstration, short lines of dancers were used and
these sometimes joined to form one line. Skips were
used to travel.

*Figure 36*

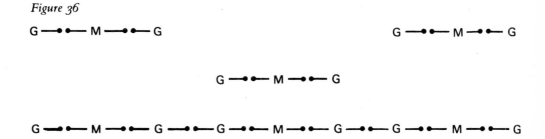

# Baidouska

Notation from Greek Folk Dances by R. Holden and M. Vouras

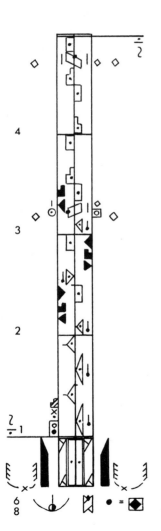

# Two Tratas of Megara

*Figure 37*

## 1 EASTER TRATA

*District*

Danced in Megara, a country town in Attica, not far from the Saronic Gulf.

*Music*

7/8 time. The dancers sing their own accompaniment.

*Style*

It is a dance for women only. The movement is flowing and continuous with a waltz–like quality.

*Formation and holds*

A chain dance which travels to the right; at the same time there is a diagonally forward and backward movement. Hands are joined in a crossed grasp; the left arm crosses in front of the neighbour's right to reach the hand of the next dancer. See figure 38. There is a slight swing in the hips to follow the pattern of the feet, but the body is upright.

| *Steps* | COUNTS |
|---|---|
| Step on R diagonally forward and to the right. | 1–3 |
| Step on L just forward of R. | 4–5 |
| Change the weight again to R with another little step. | 6–7 |
| Step on L diagonally back and to the right. | 8–10 |
| Step on R just backward of L. | 11–12 |
| Change the weight again to L with another little step. | 13–14 |

*Teaching notes*

Progress is made along a zigzag pattern with a smooth, natural turning of the hips to facilitate the diagonal stepping.

The diagonal steps are long but the weight is kept well over the feet. On the small steps the feet do not meet tidily but pass each other. Since the girls wear heeled shoes the forward diagonal step is taken on the heel, but there is no exaggeration of the action. The use of the 7 counts comes quite easily. The long step takes the extra time of 3 beats while each of the smaller steps has two beats. The effect is as of a waltz where the first step has a time stress instead of the usual extra strength.

In *The Traditional Dance* V Alford and R Gallop describe the Easter *trata* 'The trata is done only once a year on Easter Tuesday. The women gather on a dusty space at the edge of the town, where a number of wine booths have been set up for the occasion. Naturally they are wearing their finest dresses; tight-waisted, long-sleeved jackets of blue, purple or wine-coloured velvet embroidered in gold; dark pleated skirts of homespun; and brightly coloured silk petticoats. Round their necks are chains hung with their entire dowry, in gold pieces, fifty to a hundred of them, worth a couple of pounds apiece. On their heads are transparent veils of finely spun silk, covering little caps of silver coins, sewn together in the manner of chain-mail.

'Crossing their arms and linking hands as we do in Auld Lang Syne, they form into line and begin to dance, chanting their own accompaniment, a queer little oriental refrain, repeated as long as the dance lasts. First, bending forward a little, they move slowly to the right. Then straightening themselves, they take a few paces backwards. That is all there is to the dance, and it sounds very monotonous. But this very monotony makes it effective, so purposeful does it appear, and so gravely do the women, with downcast eyes play their part, as the chains serpentine among the crowd, meeting, fusing, and then going their way once more. It is hard to believe that the maidens of ancient Greece looked very different when, in silence, to the singing of the youths, they did the Chain dance in honour of Aphrodite.'[1]

*Reference*
[1] V Alford and R Gallop, *The Traditional Dance*, Methuen, 1935, page 52.

## Easter Trata

Notation by Margaret Smith from a tape recording made in Athens

*Easter Trata*

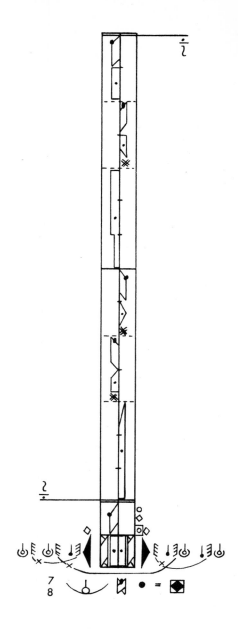

## 2 TRATA MEGARITIKI
*A dance of the fishing nets*

*Music*
In 2/4 time, stepping is even with 2 steps to the bar. The whole sequence takes 6 counts and the music is written in 6-bar phrases. To the western ear the music does not seem to match the phrasing of the dance.

*Style*
Flowing.

*Formation and holds*
The chain travels to the right. Hands are crossed as in *Easter trata*. The dancers face to the right on counts 1–2 and turn to face forward 3–6.

| *Steps* | COUNTS |
|---|---|
| 2 walks to the right beginning R. | 1–2 |
| Step sideways to the right on R turning to face forward. | 3 |
| Cross L over to touch the ground in front and to the outer side of R. | 4 |

*Figure 38*

| | |
|---|---|
| Step sideways to the left on L. | 5 |
| Cross R over to touch the ground in front and to the outer side of L. | 6 |

*Teaching notes*
The feet keep low throughout and the step has a resilient, rocking quality. The dance is made attractive, despite its simplicity, by its smooth progress and gentle, unaffected swing of the hips in response to the foot action. The dancers move as one. Many repeats are needed before dancing to the 6-bar phrase feels familiar.

*Ground pattern*
The chain travels along a loop pattern which represents the shape of the net when both ends are pulled in against the weight of the fish.

*Figure 39*

## Trata Megaritiki

Notation from *Fifty Greek Dances* by C. Sakellariou

# Trata Megaritiki

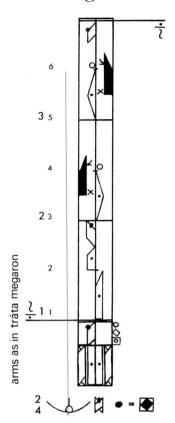

# Tsakonikos
## A DANCE OF TSAKONIA

The dance is believed to have been first danced in the island of Delos by Theseus and the Athenians to celebrate his return from the labyrinth.

*District*
Now danced in Tsakonia in the Peloponnese.

*Music*
This is in 5/8 time though it is often written in 5/4 (see kinetogram). There are two distinct sections, A and B, each reserved for its own part of the dance.

*Record*
Olympic CPTG 50000.

*Style*
A chain dance with the dancers very close together; there is a sense of unity in the group. Part A has a marked rocking quality while part B travels much more and is more vigorous. This is thought to be based on the Crane dance which Theseus and the Athenians first danced in the island of Delos to celebrate the return from the Cretan labyrinth.

*Figure 40*

*Formation and holds*
The chain faces front and travels to the right along a variety of ground patterns reminiscent of the windings of a maze. The dancers link with forearms resting on the neighbour's, left upon right, elbows bent and thumbs held. The suggestion is that this represents the holding of candles to light the way through the labyrinth  *Figure 40*

## PART A

| *Steps* | COUNTS |
|---|---|
| Step backward and a little to the right on R. | A I |
| Step forward and a little across on L. | 2 |
| Repeat 3–4 | |
| Pause on L while the right knee is drawn in behind the left knee with a smooth action. | 5 |

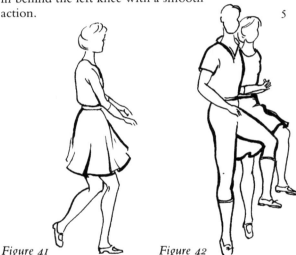

*Figure 41*          *Figure 42*

This sequence is repeated throughout the A music and a little progress is made to the right.

## PART B

| *Steps* | COUNTS |
|---|---|
| The dancers turn a little to face to the right. | |
| Step to the right and slightly backward on R. | B I |
| Step across and slightly forward on L. | 2 |
| Step to the right and slightly backward on R. | 3 |
| Hop on R while the left knee lifts  *Figure 42* | 4 |
| Step across and slightly forward on L. | 5 |

During part B the forward-backward action is less marked and much more ground is covered.

## Variations in ground patterns

*Figure 43* shows typical paths for the dancers to trace. In variation (e) the leading man changes hands to hold the next dancer, a girl, right hand to right hand to make an arch. He passes behind the line and she in front and they draw the others to dance under. When the man gets to the other end he resumes his normal hold.

## Teaching notes

In part A the feet face forward for the rocking step. When this is correctly danced the dresses of the girls move slightly forward and back, due to the marked resilience in the knees. Remember however that these are heavy, long Greek skirts and so not easily tossed to and fro. At first there may be a tendency to pause at the end of each sequence for a sixth count because the 5/8 rhythm is unfamiliar. The teacher should have the rhythm 'in her bones' so that she can lead by dancing as well as by talking the rhythm. Use the music from the beginning and leave any necessary analysis until later.

It will probably be wise to master the steps before linking in the close chain. However, as soon as some of the group knows the step the nearness of the dancers will enable them to transmit physically the feeling for the rhythm.

In part B there is no obtrusive leg gesture even when the jumping becomes vigorous.

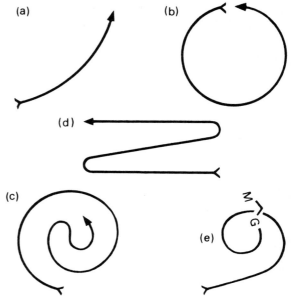

Figure 43

# Tsakonikos

Notation from *Fifty Greek Dances*, C. Sakellariou

# Tsakonikos

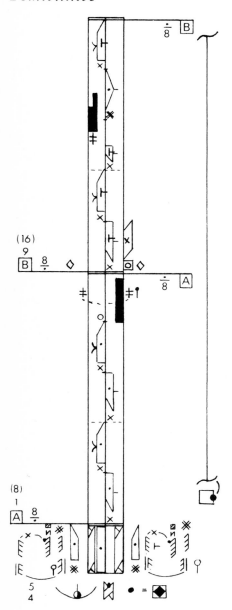

# ISRAEL

*Bat Yiftah*

*Debka Druze*

*Ta'am Haman*

# ISRAEL

In Biblical times 'Jewish dance was a prayer accompanied by music, singing, or the beating of drums' writes Sherry Rosen[1]. There is frequent reference to dancing in the Old Testament and it is clear that there were processional and ritual dances and dances of religious ecstasy. There were dances for vintage and harvest, wedding dances and dances in celebration of victory, expressing joy and praise and thanksgiving. Lilly Grove says 'Possibly no people have as yet had a dance so dignified and so grand in idea and performance as that of the Hebrews. With them it was chiefly an act of gratitude for a victory, or an accompaniment to a hymn of praise'[2]. The whole subject of these ancient dances is most fully and interestingly discussed in *The Sacred Dance* of W O E Oesterley.

In the Middle Ages Jews danced in their ghettoes, when frequent festivities encouraged gaiety and a sense of the joy of life in a people cut off from the world. Dance leaders arose to guide and organise the dancing and new dances. As a result many dancing masters of the fifteenth century were Jewish and the upsurge of dance in the Israel of today is part of a continuing tradition.

The dances of modern Israel are built in part on these Jewish foundations. Some of them are Hassidic in style with the quality of ecstasy of the early prophets; they were spontaneous, showing inner exultation and in eastern Europe in the eighteenth century they provided a means of religious and emotional expression for the masses. The Hassidim form a devout, mystical group in present day Israel.

Other dances are in the Yemenite tradition with fluid swaying action and graceful patterns of movement. The majority of Yemenite Jews came to Israel from Aden in 1949, though from the beginning of the Zionist movement they began to drift back to Palestine. In the Yemen they had been segregated and were poor and undernourished. They were, however, craftsmen with a great love of beauty which they expressed in their handwork, their poetry, songs and dances. Yemenite dance was quickly accepted as characteristic of Israel and its embroidery style is widely used for decoration.

*Debkas* with their characteristic intricate footwork and drumming rhythm are of Arab origin. The example described in this book is a *debka* of the Druze. These are a minority group in Israel, since most Druzes live in Syria and the Lebanon. They are Arab speaking and of war-like and independent spirit. They belong to an exclusive religious sect, having broken away from Islam many years ago. Joan Comay has written 'It is an exhilarating experience to be a guest at a feast in a Druze village . . . The evening is likely to culminate in a spirited *Debka*, a dance performed by the men to the accompaniment of the *oud*, a single-stringed instrument, and by the singing and clapping of the audience.'[3]

The *hora* is often called the national dance of Israel. It was brought to Israel by Jews from the Balkans, and as Gurit Kadman says, 'It fitted perfectly the pioneer character of those settlers and the social set up of the Kibbutz especially. The tightly closed circle with linked arms and hands on shoulders of the neighbours was the exact expression of the close human relationship between all members of the community. All of them with equal rights and equal value; regardless of sex or of dancing ability.'[4]

All those drawn to a new life in Israel brought dances with them and in 1944 a group of interested people began to consider the development of an Israeli dance. Unlike the other dances in this book therefore, the Israeli dances have been invented during the past thirty years. They have known choreographers and the music has often been written or adapted by modern composers. The dances have been used as one of the means of drawing people from different countries back to their common heritage. It could be claimed that these are indeed national dances and that only over the years will they reveal whether they are sufficiently well-rooted to merit the title of folk dances.

The first of the dance festivals was held at the kibbutz in Dalia in 1944. The enthusiasm which it aroused led to the creating of many new dances and of these the best have survived. 'The new dances spread to the towns and cities as well and conquered the youth, helped to integrate the new immigrants in the life of the country, shaped the character of big celebrations like Independence Day, and were also received enthusiastically by Jews all over the world who quickly took to them as a means of identification with the new Israeli culture,' writes Mrs Kadman, while Rivka Sturman adds, 'I believe that those dances which have our rhythm and faithfully express our search for origin in dance and music will last'[5].

### Style and types of dance

The Israeli dances have developed for the most part as social dances. There are a few with an element of mimetic action such as *mayim, mayim* where the movement symbolises the drawing of water from the well, and *el ginat egoz* (the nut garden) in which the finger position signifies the holding of a nut for the girl. The dances were often first performed at festivals in village and settlement, but soon lost their special festive or ritual significance and were absorbed as dances of every day, a substitute for ballroom dances.

Many of them are circle dances, derived from the *hora*, but with a new exuberance appropriate to a people inspired to make a fresh start in a land of difficulty as well as of opportunity. The Yemenite dances are often couple dances with a lyrical quality, many are love dances. Hassidic dances have retained something of the sense of inner emotion characteristic of the Hassidic sect, while *debkas* are line dances with an exciting pounding, rhythmic nature, danced chiefly by men.

### Costume

Just as a new nation has no dances of its own, so it has no traditional dress. Gurit Kadman in a most interesting booklet, *The New Israeli Folkdance*, speaks of efforts to establish a costume suitable for dancing, 'There have been many attempts . . . to create an original and specific attire of our own for holiday and folk dance. But here again we should not have any illusions; we cannot force upon people our idea of festive garments; we can only offer suggestions and hope that people will like and wear them—though the mere idea of developing national costume now-a-days seems illusory'[6]. At an early stage in the development of the dances an attempt was made, through a competition, to find a suitable design and doubtless the results influenced some of the groups in their choice of a costume. It is to the Yemenite tradition that most dancers seem to have turned in designing their costumes. The girls wear dresses with full skirts, embellished with Yemenite embroidery;

the bell-shaped sleeves and the neckline of the bodice are also embroidered. Both sleeves and skirt may be slit to allow for greater freedom of movement. The men wear trousers of a similar material, frequently a tough cotton, with a loose, straight over-shirt, again embroidered at neck and sleeves. Gay colours are chosen and the dress sets off the movements of the dance. The costume is simple and the dancers are bare-footed or wear light sandals.

In Israel it is possible to buy postcards of folk dance groups. The costumed dolls are beautifully made and excellently dressed, giving a sense of the Israeli character as well as a good idea of the clothes.

### Music

Most of the dances are named by the title of their music and the movement is inspired by the tune. The pattern of the dance does not, however, usually relate closely to the words of the dance-song since, 'Most dances have no specific theme, but express joy of life and of collective motion and exuberance of youth'[7]. Nevertheless Anat Keren in teaching *ta'am haman* said 'The words give extra meaning to the dance', suggesting that they enhanced the lyric mood of the movement.

A difficulty arises if the dancers sing words in English translation to the tunes of Hebrew songs since the stress may be placed in a way which detracts from the meaning. Interestingly a similar difficulty arises in Israel itself in the singing of traditional songs. It is discussed by Karol Salomon in an article entitled *Problems of old songs in a revived language*. He observes that the changed accents of modern Hebrew render many traditional songs meaningless. The teacher should take pains with the singing and if possible the dancers should sing in Hebrew. It is likely that Jews living in the neighbourhood would be willing to advise, or that a local dance club would come to demonstrate and teach both dance and song.

The dances are often accompanied also by the clapping of hands by both dancers and audience. Frequently the music begins in a slow and steady manner and, following the acceleration of the dancers, builds to a climax, retaining always the compelling inner pulse.

The mixture of eastern and western influences poses a special problem in regard to suitable instruments to accompany the dancers. The music of a mixed orchestra is more satisfying than that of the widely used accordion. The different types of dance need contrasting accompaniment. The rousing *horas* are often sung to the music of violins, accordions, mouth organs and guitars, whereas woodwind suits the slightly melancholy tunes of some of the Yemenite dances and together with drum-beating provides a good accompaniment to the strange pulsing of the *debkas*. The stirring, urgent quality of much Israeli dance music makes an immediate appeal to young people; though rooted in tradition it is essentially modern in spirit.

### References
1 Sherry Rosen, 'The Story of Jewish Dance', *Viltis Folklore Magazine*, Volume 27, Number 3, 1968
2 Lilly Grove, *Dancing*, Longman's Green and Co, 1895, page 24
3 Joan Comay, *Introducing Israel*, Methuen and Co, London, 1963, page 57
4 Gurit Kadman, *The New Israeli Folk Dance*, 1968, page 3
5 Gurit Kadman, *The New Israeli Folk Dance*, 1968, page 8 and
   Rivka Sturman, *Ten Folk Dances for All Ages*, Tel Aviv, 1962, page
6 Gurit Kadman, *The New Israeli Folk Dance*, 1968, page 16
7 As 6 above, page 12.

### Source of the dances
The three dances which are included were taught by Anat Keren during a visit to England, when a filmed record was made of these and several other dances.

### Acknowledgment
Most sincere appreciation is recorded for the help given by:
Miss Anat Keren of Ashdod
Mrs Hannah Popovsky of the Wingate Institute, Tel Aviv
Mrs Debra Marcus of the Physical Education Department, Hebrew University, Jerusalem
Miss Naomi Stamelman and Mr Igal Perry of the Bat-Dor Dance Company, who supplied the kinetograms
Mr and Mrs Jacob Barkan

### Bibliography
*The Sacred Dance*, W O E Oesterley, Cambridge University Press, 1923
*The New Israeli Folk Dances*, Gurit Kadman, 1968
*A Jewish Dancing Master of the Renaissance*, Otto Kinkeldey, Dance Horizons, New York, 1929
*Introducing Israel*, Joan Comay, Methuen and Co, London, 1963
*Folk Tales of Israel*, Editor Dov Noy, Routledge and Kegan Paul, London, 1963
'The Making of Music', Yohanan Boehm, *Israel Today* Number 12, Jerusalem, 1966 and University of Chicago Press
'The Story of Jewish Dance', Sherry Rosen, *Viltis Folklore Magazine*, Volume 27, Number 3, 1968

The following books of dances are available from the Physical Education Association, 10 Nottingham Place, London WC1
*Ten Folk Dances for all Ages*, Rivka Sturman, Tel Aviv, 1962
*Ten Israeli Folk Dances*, G Kadman and T Hodes, Education and Culture Centre of the General Federation of Labour in Israel, 1959

### Sources of information
Embassy of Israel, 2 Palace Green, London W8
Israel Government Tourist Office, 59 St James's Street, SW1
Israel in London Shop, New Oxford Street, London WC1

### Opportunities to see dancing
In Israel the chief dance festival is held at Dalia in August, but there are a number of other festivals where dances play a less important part and there are opportunities to see the dance companies whose work is based in the Yemenite tradition.

Those who visit Israel for a working holiday on a Kibbutz will have plenty of opportunity to join in the dancing, and will be astonished at the capacity of the Israelis for dancing for hours on end. The Academy Travel Agency, New Oxford Street, arranges for parties to travel abroad to see folk dance and recently planned two such visits to Israel. In Britain there are a number of lively Jewish groups in the big towns who practise the dances.

### Records
There are very many records of Israeli dances and they are reasonably easy to obtain. Care should be taken in selecting them that the tempo is correct for dancing. In USA where there is a very great interest in the dances, a large number of recordings has been made.
*Israel Folk Dance Party*, Makolit, Tel Aviv, LP 12004
*Folk Songs and Dances*, Karmon Israeli Dancers and Singers, Vanguard AN 63–97
*Israeli Folk Dances*, Efi Netzer, Hakalit Haifa HI 30010

*This is Israel* Recorded in Haifa, issued by Marble Arch Mal 1138

*Folk Dances of Israel*, CBS Israel Orchestra, CBS Israel 62975

The following and many others are available from the USA:

*Tikva* T 24, T 69, T 98

*Folkraft* LP 12 recorded in Israel

## SOME ISRAELI STEPS

*Israeli walk*

This takes two distinct counts. On the first R is placed forward and on the second or off beat the right knee bends a little, while L lifts so that the weight is fully transferred to R. The effect is one of slight syncopation.

*Teaching* Try to avoid all exaggeration. If used without undue stress words are helpful,

STEP-GIVE-STEP-GIVE

Though distinct the two parts of the step have continuity; there should be no sudden or strong knee bend. If the dancers begin to accent the bend of the knee too strongly, it helps to return to an ordinary walking step and then gradually to introduce the merest suggestion of easing the knee on the second count. Humming the tune will be useful.

*Grapevine*

As its name suggests this is a twining step. It travels sideways. In dancing to the left, R crosses in front of L (1), then L steps to the side (2), R crosses again this time behind L (3), and L steps again to the side (4).

*Teaching* The dancers will quickly get the feeling of the step if the teacher joins hands with them in a circle stepping slowly and counting,

ACROSS IN FRONT—TO THE SIDE—ACROSS BEHIND—
TO THE SIDE

and gradually building to the rhythm and tempo of the music,

CROSS-SIDE-CROSS-SIDE

FRONT-SIDE-BACK-SIDE

Then a short practice with the dancers all facing the same direction, the teacher out in front with her back to the group, will enable the dancers to copy exactly and ensure that all are confident.

Stress should be laid on good poise and the maintenance of the forward direction of the body even though the hips turn to follow the twining pattern of the feet. A slight turn out of the crossing foot will help to maintain the forward-facing position of the dancer. Resilience in knees and ankles is needed to produce a flowing action. Singing will also help the dancers to acquire the flowing style.

A usual variation of this step is to stress the fourth count by a leap. In this the sense of lift should come through the body and not as the result of an athletic thrust from feet and legs.

## Yemenite

This step is smooth and flowing; the dancer faces front and there is just a little sway of the shoulders to follow the path of the movement. The first step is to the side on R (1), then L closes up behind and a little across R (2) and R steps diagonally forward and across (3).

*Teaching* The teacher will find that the dancers learn easily if she demonstrates facing them, inviting them to join in. The teacher dances with the opposite foot to that used by the class which thus has a mirror picture to copy. The step may also be practised holding hands in a line; this helps the dancers to feel the wave-like action. Count (2) is often danced as a small side step, instead of a crossing.

The stepping is resilient and the transfer of weight on the second count is lilting and without emphasis; this closing of the feet is not exact.

The step is often danced in duple time. Then the fourth count is taken for a pause, during which the front knee straightens and there is a gentle lift through the body. In other dances there is a slight hop on the fourth count.

# Bat Yiftah
## JEPHTAH'S DAUGHTER*

*Music*
4/4 time. The interest lies in the dancer's stress of the off beat. There are three sections to the music which correspond to the three parts of the dance.

*Record*
Makolit LP 12004

*Style*
A couple dance. Part A is contained and pulsing, whilst parts B and C have a sense of swinging and travelling over the ground.

### PART A
*Formation and holds*
The girl is at her partner's right side and the couple dances cc round the room. Left hands are joined at chest height with the girl's elbow well bent; right hands are joined and held behind the girl's right shoulder.

| *Steps* | COUNTS |
|---|---|
| 2 Israeli walks forward R, L. | A 1–2, 3–4 |
| Hopping on L make 2 brushing gestures with R in which the whole foot moves in a forward direction so that the ball brushes along the ground in a forward direction and the knee is then withdrawn with an upward circling which leads into the repeat of the brush. | 5–8 |

*Figure 44*

*See *Old Testament* Judges 11 verses 30–40

*Figure 44*

2 Israeli walks forward R, L.                    9–10, 11–12
Hopping on L make 1 brush gesture and
then place R beside L taking no weight.          13–16
Dance the whole sequence once more.

## PART B
*Formation and holds*
The same grasp as in part A is used throughout,
including the pivot. The dancers continue to travel cc.

| Steps | COUNTS |
|---|---|
| 2 runs forward R, L. | B 1, 2 |
| Spring on both feet together. | 3 |
| Spring again on L with R lifted slightly backward. | 4 |

*Figure 45*

This short sequence is repeated.                     5–8
The couple turns about cc with 3 pivots
on R and finishes facing LOD with a
spring on both feet followed by a
spring on L with R lifted backward.        9–14, 15, 16

## PART C
*Formations and holds*
The dancers separate. The man dances to the centre
of the room while the girl dances behind him. Then
he dances back away from the centre and she comes
round to face him. A waist grasp with the right arm
across in front of the partner is used for the pivot in
this part of the dance. The free arm is held out
sideways with the palm of the hand facing up.

| Steps | COUNTS |
|---|---|
| MAN | |
| He dances to the centre clapping his hands on the off beat. | |
| 4 Israeli walks beginning R. | C 1–8 |
| *Figure 47.* | |
| 4 Israeli walks backward still clapping. | 9–16 |
| Step sideways R, close L to R with a clap. | 17–18, 19–20 |
| Step sideways L, close R to L with a clap. | 21–22, 23–24 |
| 4 pivots round with partner. | 25–32 |

*Figure 46*

GIRL

As the man leaves her she continues to
pivot with her knuckles at her waist.
4 pivots on R turning to the right on
the spot.                                          C 1-8
*Figure 47*
Facing the centre cc to own right.
2 runs R to side, L across in front of R.          9, 10
Spring on both feet still travelling.              11
Spring on R with L lifted a little to
the side.                                          12
*Figure 47*
Still facing the centre and travelling to
own left.
2 runs L to side, R across in front of L.          13, 14
Spring on both feet still travelling.              15
Spring again on L lifting R a little
backward and preparing to travel to the
centre.                                            16
*Figure 47.*
4 runs forward beginning R and
passing by the man's left side.                    17-20
4 runs swinging round to face the man.             21-24
*Figure 47.*
4 pivots on R with right arm round
partner's waist.                                   25-32
Dance the whole sequence once more.

*Teaching notes*

In part A the accent is forward in the brushing gesture.
The knee is not lifted very high on the recovery. A
little give in the supporting knee helps in stressing the
forward brush.

The steps of part B travel forward rather than up,
and again the feet are not lifted high, but the steps are
springy and lively. The pivot also travels; there is no
tidy closing of the feet. Note that each pivot step takes
2 counts.

The girl covers a lot of ground in part C and her
whole sequence should join up smoothly. She must
master a number of rapid changes of direction with
control but without losing the free-flowing character
of the movement. The pivot in this section is danced
with the right sides close together. The man enjoys
clapping the rhythm as he waits for the girl.

For successful dancing it is necessary to give much
attention to ensuring easy changes from one part of
the dance to the next and especially back to the
beginning again.

(c) PART C  Counts 13 - 16

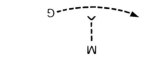

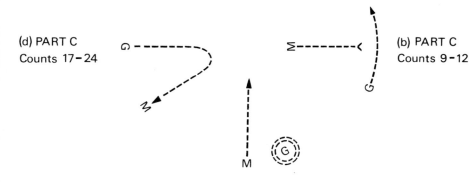

(d) PART C
Counts 17 - 24

(b) PART C
Counts 9 - 12

*Figure 47*                        (a) PART C  Counts 1 - 8

## Bat Yiftah

*Music* Amitai Ne'eman
*Dance* Shalom Hermon

# Bat Yiftah

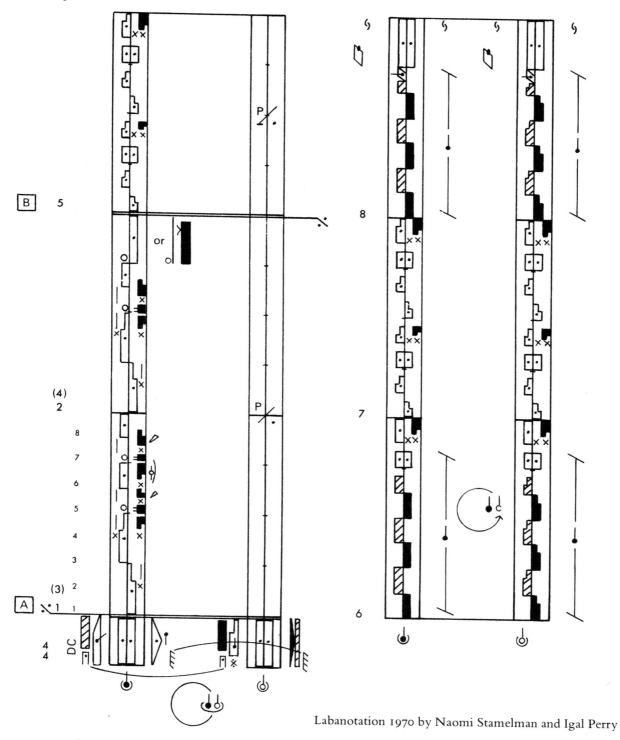

Labanotation 1970 by Naomi Stamelman and Igal Perry

DC = dancer's counts        P = partner

# Bat Yiftah

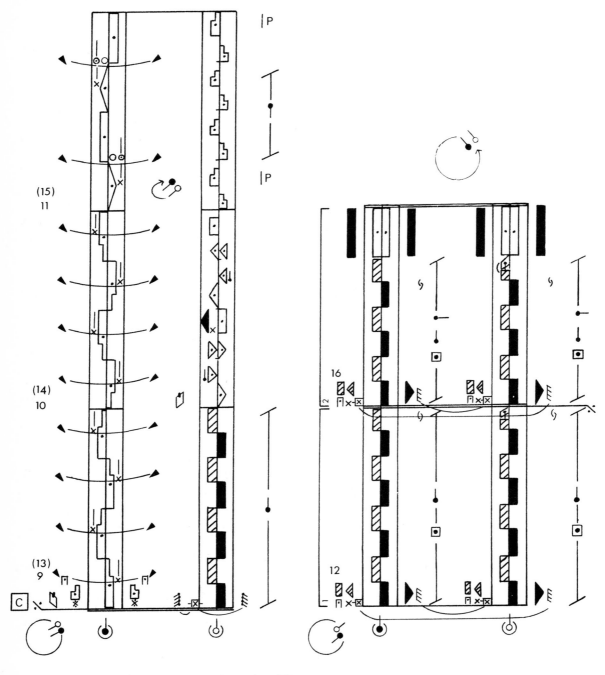

Labanotation 1970 by Naomi Stamelman and Igal Perry

# Debka Druze

Many *debkas* are danced by men only but women also dance this *debka* of the Druze. The first version which is described is as danced by Anat Keren; the second version which follows a very similar pattern is as demonstrated by Jacob Barkan. This second version is more authentic though when danced by girls the style of the first is often used.

## Music
4/4 time with a well marked rhythm. It is usual for *debkas* to be accompanied by drums only during part of the dance. Since *debkas* are dances of horsemen the rhythm is reminiscent of pounding hooves. The music is in two sections which correspond to part A and part B of the dance; each takes 16 bars of music. Part A of the dance is used as a chorus and is repeated between each step variation.

## Record
Makolit LP 12004

## Style
The steps are staccato and stop fractionally in position. There is a constant slight bounce, a pulsing, in the knees. Heads are held high and the body vertical with weight well over the base.

## Formation and holds
A chain dance in which the hands are held low and the dancers are very close together with bodies almost touching. This means that movements must be exact, eg feet should be lifted to the same height. There is a small, subtle twist and shrug of the shoulders. The leading man raises his free hand, rather like a flag, to guide the others.

A slightly different hand hold is adopted in Version B, though the dancers are still close together. The left forearm is placed horizontally across the dancer's back at waist level; the dancer behind reaches forward with the right hand to form the chain.

VERSION A (often danced by women)
## PART A

| Steps | COUNTS |
|---|---|
| 2 Israeli walks L, R. | A 1–2, 3–4 |
| Point left toe forward, hold. | 5, 6 |
| Point left toe backward and slightly outward, hold. | 7, 8 |

Figure 48

Dance this sequence 3 times more.

## PART B

| Steps | COUNTS |
|---|---|
| Hop on R as the left toe is crossed behind the right calf with knee turned out, hold. | B 1, 2 |

Figure 49

Hop again R as L lifts to side with toe
turned up, hold.                                    3, 4

*Figure 50*

Touch the ground with the left heel.               5
Leap on to L in the place of R which lifts
slightly backward.                                  6
Quickly put R beside L, hold.                       7, 8
Dance this sequence 3 times more.

## PART A
Danced as before.

## PART C
*Steps*                                             COUNTS
Step forward L, hold.                               B 1, 2
Close R beside L, hold.                             3, 4
Step sideways to left on L, hold.                   5, 6
Close R to L but transfer no weight,
hold.                                               7, 8
Leap sideways on to R as the left toe
crosses behind the right calf with the
knee turned out, hold.                              9, 10
Hop on R as L lifts to the side with toe
turned up, hold.                                    11, 12
Touch the ground with the left heel.               13
Quickly put L in the place of R which
lifts slightly backward.                            14
Quickly put R beside L, hold.                       15, 16
Dance this sequence once more.

## PART A
Danced as before.

## PART D
*Steps*                                             COUNTS
Left heel beats the ground ahead, hold.            B 1, 2
Leap on L in place of R which lifts
slightly backward.                                  3
Quickly put R beside L.                             4
Repeat this short sequence.                         5–8
2 high springy jumps on the spot with
feet stretching.                                    9–10, 11–12
Repeat the short sequence (counts 1–4)
again.                                              13–16
Dance the whole sequence once more.

## PART A
Danced as before.

## PART E
*Steps*                                             COUNTS
Leap on L turning about to face back
along the line, hold.                               B 1, 2
Bring R round beside L but transfer no
weight, hold. The body crouches a little
over the bent knees.                                3, 4

*Figure 51*

Carry the right knee in a big circle to
step R back in place facing LOD. The
body rises to the erect.                            5–6
Bring L to R patting the ground with the
whole foot but transferring no weight,
hold.                                               7, 8
Dance this sequence 3 more times.

## PART A
Danced as before.

*Teaching notes*

All the holds are marked by a little bounce in the knee of the supporting leg. There is need for great accuracy both in timing and in foot placing. Master the steps before joining in the close chain. The teacher should prepare word guidance for each variation and should say the words in the clipped staccato manner of the movement, eg

LEFT–HOLD–CLOSE–HOLD–SIDE–HOLD–CLOSE–AND
LEAP–HOLD–HEEL–HOLD–TOUCH–CHANGE–
DOWN–HOLD

for part C.

Each part alternating with the chorus may be used as a little dance and may be repeated many times so that the dancers may enjoy the rhythm before going on to memorize all the parts.

## VERSION B (as danced by men)
### PART A
*Steps*                                          COUNTS

Instead of pointing the ball of foot touches the ground very slightly in advance of R.                        5, 6

With slight outward rotation the ball touches slightly behind the level of R.               7, 8
In both cases the foot is almost flat on the floor.
The shoulder opens and the head turns slightly to the left.

### PART B
*Steps*                                          COUNTS

The dancer jumps on to R moving slightly sideways to the right with a sense of overbalancing and at the same time lifts the left heel to rest against the right calf.                                        1, 2
There is a sense of stamping in this step.

### PART C
*Steps*

On counts 9, 10 the action is as described in Part B of this version.

## PART D
*Steps*

Following the two springs (9–12) the dancer moves forward with 3 lightly stamped steps R, L, R, rounding the back to a crouching position.

## PART E
For this part a thumb grasp is used. Dancers grasp the left thumb of the neighbour.

*Steps*                                          COUNTS

L is placed slightly forward on the heel.        1
L steps beside R.                                2
Then the line turns slightly to the left so that the dancers change from a file to be side by side.
R then leaps across to the outer side of L and L lifts.                                     3, 4
Weight is transferred back to L.                 5, 6
Right knee makes a big circle and R takes the weight again facing forward with the dancers once again in a file.       7, 8

*Teaching notes*

As for Version A but there is even more sense of pounding with some beating by the feet.
In Part E the leap across is into a deep position.
Throughout there is a slight sense of outward rotation in the moving leg.

## Debka Druze

*Dance* Samuel Cohen
*Music* Uri Giv'on

# Debka Druze

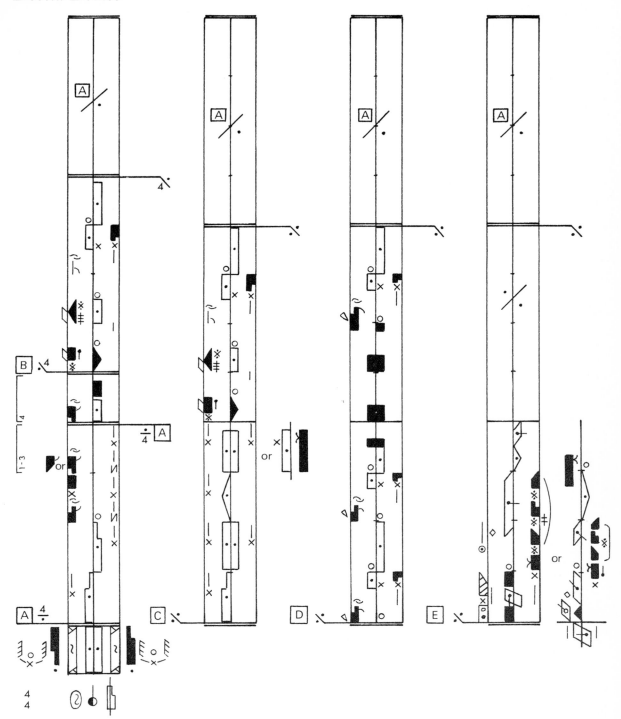

Labanotation 1970 by Naomi Stamelman and Igal Perry

## Ta'am Haman
### THE TASTE OF MANNA

*Music*

This is a love song and the dancers should sing as they dance. The music is in a swinging 3/4 time. Each part of the dance takes 16 bars of music. The music is based on a Persian melody.

*Records*

Makolit LP 12004   Vanguard AN 63–97   Tikva T 69

*Style*

A couple dance which is lilting in quality. The steps cover the ground in a smooth swinging way with a sense of rocking.

## PART A1
*Formation and holds*

The girl is at her partner's right side; they face cc. They join hands in a crossed grasp (skaters' hold) just above waist height.

| Steps | COUNTS |
|---|---|
| Step to the left on L, close R behind. | A 1–2, 3 |
| Step L diagonally across and forward. | 4–6 |
| (The above is the timing of the Yemenite step throughout this dance.) | |
| Step through and rock forward on R. | 7–9 |
| Rock back on to L. | 10–12 |
| Repeat the rocking forward and back. | 13–18 |
| Repeat the Yemenite step starting on R. | 19–24 |
| Dance the whole sequence once more. | |

## PART B1
*Formation and holds*

Partners retain the crossed grasp. They now travel sideways first moving towards the centre of the room and then away.

| Steps | COUNTS |
|---|---|
| Step to the left on L, close R to L. | B 1–2,3 |
| Step again to the side on L. | 4–6 |
| Bending the left knee swing R across with a heel lead to just below knee height. | 7–9 |
| Bend the left knee again with a smooth rebounding action and mark count 10 with a little downward movement of the right heel. | 10–12 |

*Figure 52*

| | COUNTS |
|---|---|
| Repeat this sequence starting on R and travelling away from the centre. | 13–24 |
| Repeat the whole sequence once more. | |

## PART C1
*Formation and holds*

Still in the crossed grasp but now travelling LOD cc.

| Steps | COUNTS |
|---|---|
| 1 small yemenite step beginning L. | C 1–6 |
| Step forward R bringing the leg through with a swinging circling of the knee. | 7–8 |
| *Figure 55.* | |
| Small step forward L. | 9 |
| Step forward R. | 10–12 |
| Repeat the sequence 3 more times. | |

## PART A2
*Formation and holds*

Partners face each other. The man has his back to the centre. He clasps the girl's right hand in both of his at about chest height.

*Figure 53*

*Figure 54*

*Steps*                                    COUNTS

Repeat the steps of A1. Partners separate
slightly on the Yemenite steps and are
opposite each other for the rocking
which brings them toward each other
and away.                          D 1–24, 1–24


## PART B2
*Formation and holds*

The man still has his back to the centre and the girl
faces him. Each travels sideways along the circle first
to the left and then back again. Arms are free and
swing in response to the action of the feet.

*Steps*                                    COUNTS

Repeat the steps of B1. As the dancers
travel to the left they leave each other;
when they travel to the right they move
back to face each other. The arms lift
easily sideways on the travelling; as the
supporting knee bends (count 10) the
opposite arm swings across so that the
dancer meets the neighbour's hand with
a gentle clap. On the return the
partners clap.                     E 1–24, 1–24

## PART C2
*Formation holds and steps*                COUNTS
Repeat C1 exactly.                 C 1–24, 1–24


*Teaching notes*

In part A the rocking has a scooping shape. The
Yemenite step is fluent and lilting but the foot
placings are not exact.

In part B the leg is bent and swings across with a
sweeping gesture. The heel leads and the toe is *not*
pointed. Resilience in the supporting knee ensures a
bouncing and not a jerky movement. The little
emphasis (count 10) is a tiny but firm downward
pressure of the heel made in the air just below knee
height. In B2 the arm comes across for the clap as the
result of a body turn.

In part C the Yemenite step is always to the left
which produces a slightly zigzag path. The weight is
gently dropped on to the left foot in this particular
Yemenite step. Then the right leg is brought through
for the travelling with quite a large lifting and turning
gesture which seems almost to have spring. This
travelling step is like a polka, counted

LIFT–LONG–SHORT–LONG

See Figure 56.

In preparing for c2 the dancers retain the hand contact of the clap, join the right hands also and swing into the travelling step.

*Figure 55*

# Ta'am Haman

*Music* I. E. Navon
*Dance* Yoav Ashriel

# Ta'am Haman

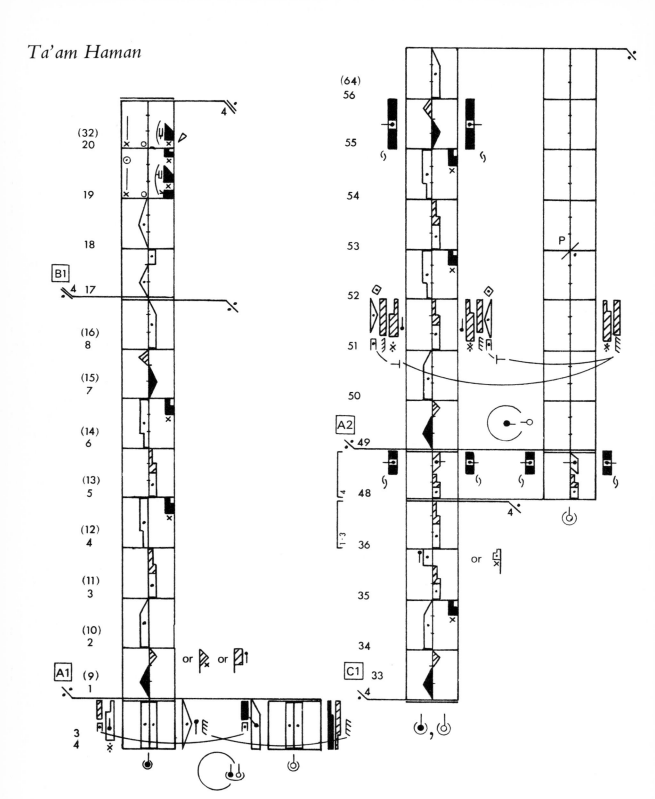

# Ta'am Haman

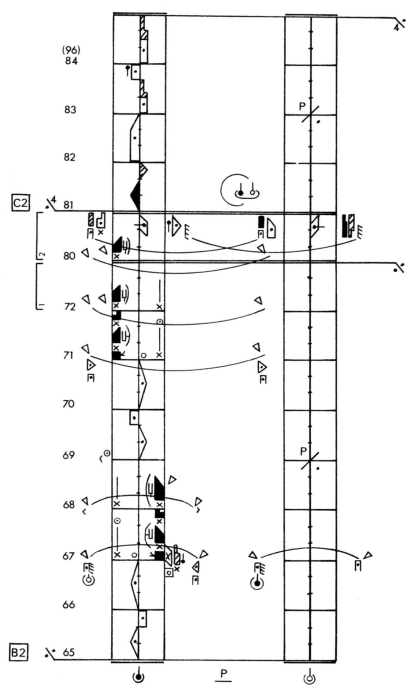

Labanotation 1970 by Naomi Stamelman and Igal Perry

# INDEX

Names of dances appear in *italics*